Work of God

Benedictine Prayer

Judith Sutera, O.S.B.
Editor

A Liturgical Press Book

THE LITURGICAL PRESS
Collegeville, Minnesota

1   2   3   4   5   6   7   8   9

Library of Congress Cataloging-in-Publication Data

Work of God : Benedictine prayer / Judith Sutera, editor.
      p.   cm.
  ISBN 0-8146-2431-6
  1. Benedictines—Spiritual life. 2. Benedictines—Prayer-books and devotions—English. I. Sutera, Judith.
BX3003.W67   1997
242'.6942—dc21   96-51704
                                                CIP

Contents

Diana Scamman
4821 SW Urish Rd.
Topeka, KS 66610-9667

FOREWORD

Benedictine prayer is not something to be done only by people in monasteries. It is deeply rooted in the Judeo-Christian tradition and has been used by countless people. The Liturgical Press has fostered that tradition throughout this century by publishing a series of "Manuals for Oblates of St. Benedict." This book continues that tradition, but with a title which reflects that one need not be an oblate to use the monastic Liturgy of the Hours. Although the texts used in this book are not yet officially approved for use in the liturgy, we hope *Work of God: Benedictine Prayer* will be a rich sampler for beginners and a useful companion for those already praying in this way.

Why publish another book of the Divine Office when there are numerous prayer books available to the public? The primary reason is that this one is rooted in the Benedictine monastic version of the Office. It is modified from St. Benedict's directives, but has them as its foundation. The themes and language have a markedly Benedictine flavor, and additional materials on Benedictine spirituality have been included.

While there are other translations of the psalms and Scripture which may have been used, we have had to make certain editorial decisions. The ICEL translation of the psalms has been many years in the making and was carefully prepared by a group of highly qualified scholars. We have attempted to be as inclusive as possible, and to praise God with diverse images and titles. In the New Revised Standard Version of the Bible, which has been used for the readings, the word "LORD" frequently appears. This is a convention used to denote the unspeakable name of God in the Hebrew texts and has a meaning far beyond that of a ruler of subjects.

Much of the work of selecting antiphons and texts for the Liturgy of the Hours in this book was done by Joan Wingert, O.S.B., whose invaluable contributions must be acknowledged with deep gratitude. Irene Nowell, O.S.B., was also a great help by both her knowledge and her encouragement. This work is a gift to all the oblates of Mount St. Scholastica, Atchison, Kansas, who have helped in so many ways to open my eyes to a greater appreciation of Benedictine spirituality.

Judith Sutera, O.S.B.
Editor

THE LIFE AND THE SPIRIT OF ST. BENEDICT

The Benedictine way of life has one of the longest life-spans of any institution in Western civilization. It traces its roots to the life of Benedict of Norcia, who was born around 480. The spirituality which Benedict espoused, however, is rooted in gospel values and in a way of expressing these values which was already known in Benedict's time as the monastic life.

The monastic life exists in many forms and in many other cultures. From the earliest days of Christianity, there had been those who desired to give up all personal possessions and gains and to devote themselves entirely to a radical Christian witness. Some lived in isolation or engaged in severe feats of self-discipline in order to focus the mind and body more totally on the transcendent. Some formed groups to live the common life as idealized in the accounts of the Christian communities of the apostles' time. By the fifth century there were many such persons. Benedict did not invent Christian monasticism, but he did much to articulate and foster it.

What is known about Benedict's life comes primarily from stories of his life which were gathered and written down by Pope St. Gregory the Great in the 590s. They appeared as Book II of a four-part work entitled *The Dialogues*. Benedict is the centerpiece for numerous stories of local saints, intended to provide heroes for the struggling Italian people.

According to the stories, based on accounts by those who had known him, Benedict was sent as a youth to be educated in Rome where the decline and invasion of the empire was well under way. He left the city and became a hermit, but eventually came forth to teach and influence those living in the vicinity. Followers gathered, and he began a monastic community at Subiaco, later moving to Monte Cassino. He was reported to have had a sister, Scholastica, who also lived the monastic life nearby with a group of women. There are many stories of miracles and wise insight, of threats to his life because of his goodness and honesty, of his own struggles in the quest for God. Towards the end of his life, he wrote a summary of his thoughts on the monastic life which is known today as the *Rule of St. Benedict.*

The Rule was based on earlier monastic instructions, but had a tone which was distinctively Benedict's. He tempers much of the emphasis on sinfulness and frailty which was prevalent in his primary source, known only as the *Rule of the Master.* He encourages moderation in discipline and adaptation to the uniqueness of individuals. He begins with a fear (reverent awe) of God but emphasizes that the aim of the rigors and self-knowledge is to develop a love which casts out fear.

He does not encourage his followers to extraordinary acts of self-punishment, but to a self-discipline in all the ordinary circumstances of life. Benedict focuses on a self-awareness and God-awareness which form the individual both in action and in interior disposition. If one is always conscious of the presence of God, and of God's knowledge of all actions and thoughts, then all of life can be transformed into a modeling of the peaceable kingdom of God. Hospitality is a hallmark of Benedictinism because one is to learn to see God in every other person, especially the most needy or unattractive. Good stewardship and ecological consciousness have long been associated with the Benedictine way simply because one is to perceive every tool, every item or talent used, as holy in the sight of God and as pure gift from God.

The person who would live in the spirit of St. Benedict is one who is always alert to God. The opening word of the Rule, "listen," is its essence. One listens first of all to the words of Scripture which teach God's way. The day is framed by periods of prayer which take on the rhythms of night and day, feast and fast, celebration and sorrow, and make each sacred. These are reinforced by periods of personal reflection, traditionally referred to as *lectio*. This practice can take various forms, but is a time when one allows the Word to speak within the self in an environment of silence and solitude.

One also grows in the ability to hear the Word in others. Benedict recognized that the individual is shaped by community and so he devoted much attention to the way in which a person interacts with others. Relationships with superiors are to model one's relationship with God. Those who are in authority must likewise guide as God would guide. All those who would live as Christians are expected to live as the early Christian community lived, as Christ taught, and as people who truly love and revere one another. Benedict also recognized that persons influence one another for good or evil and are a primary resource in the search for God.

For Benedict, seeking God must necessarily lead one to listen to one's self, to recognize God in this unique work of creation with all honesty and bring it to its ultimate fulfillment. The journey on which

Benedict takes the reader, through the steps of grow-
ing humility of heart, is rigorous, but wrapped in
the compassion of God and in a great optimism about
its outcome. Disciples of Benedict are encouraged to
abandon self-centeredness and to see the weakness
and sinfulness that is in them. Yet they are not left at
this stage of awareness. In seeing one's own small-
ness, one can grow to a greater appreciation of the
largeness of God's power and love and mercy. It is in
this understanding that the person can truly love the
self as it really is, love the other as a manifestation of
God, and love God as the source and center of all of
life.

Life is thus unified and made sacred. A Benedictine spirituality, like any gospel-based way of life, is a
living recognition that God is present, that Jesus has
conquered evil and death, that the reign of God on
earth has begun. It is also a witness that the fulfillment
of the kingdom is nearer whenever very diverse people
can live together in peace and love. This can happen,
however, only through the internal transformation of
individual persons, families, or communities. Benedict would have all people learn to turn away from
those things which are self-serving and turn towards
the relentless pursuit of holiness. Gregory summarizes
the quest in a vision which Benedict is said to have
had towards the end of his life:

> In the dead of night he suddenly beheld a flood of
> light shining down from above more brilliant than
> the sun, and with it every trace of darkness cleared
> away. . . . According to his own description, the
> whole world was gathered up before his eyes in what
> appeared to be a single ray of light.

[Gregory explains] All creation is bound to appear small to a soul that sees the Creator. Once it beholds a little of God's light, it finds all creatures small indeed. The light of holy contemplation enlarges and expands the mind in God until it stands above the world. In fact, the soul that sees God rises even above itself, and as it is drawn upward in God's light all its inner powers unfold. Then, when it looks down from above, it sees how small everything really is that was beyond its grasp before.

Judith Sutera, O.S.B.

BENEDICTINISM AND
THE WORLD AROUND IT:
THE OBLATE MOVEMENT

From its beginnings Benedictinism has touched the lives of many people beyond those who dwell in monasteries. While Benedict encouraged separation for the sake of quiet and contemplation, a life ordered to spiritual practices, his community was not an escape from a world perceived as hopelessly evil. Rather, it was like a family which has its own customs and privacy, but which interacts to some degree with its neighbors.

In the biography of St. Benedict, the second book of Pope Gregory the Great's *Dialogues,* the people nearby came and "gave him the food of the body and took back, in turn, the spiritual sustenance of life which they had received from his lips." Other portions tell of visits by priests and kings, instruction of nuns and villagers, and works of charity to the sick, hungry, impoverished, and captive. Theoprobus, a nobleman, enjoyed Benedict's "deep and trusting friendship" and is described as having access to Benedict's cell.

The life of a region could not help but be transformed by such a presence as Benedict. If people were converted by the teaching of Benedict, they would most probably have incorporated not only the Christian message, but Benedict's own interpretation of these values, into their lives.

There seems to have been not only a broad relationship of monastery to neighborhood, but some kind of specific relationship between Benedict's community and particular individuals such as those mentioned above. While the word "oblate" originally referred to a child offered by parents for religious life, some children apparently were educated in a monastery, or elsewhere by monastic tutors, but did not remain in religious life. This was true of members of royalty such as Charlemagne and Louis the Pious. This early influence would have affected perceptions of the world and, at least in these two cases, resulted in special concern for the preservation and promulgation of Benedict's Rule.

Most noteworthy is Duke Henry II of Bavaria, Holy Roman Emperor and saint of the early 11th century, now honored as a special patron of Benedictine oblates. He is described as having supported the monastic life and participated devoutly in liturgy whenever possible. When made emperor in 1002, he sent his insignia to Cluny. He finally succeeded in getting a monastery to accept him, but its abbot commanded him in obedience to continue ruling.

Even earlier, there is mention in various sources of persons or families living in communities near monasteries. It is difficult in these early examples of lay participation to identify just what was the relationship to the monastery. Feudal monasteries would have necessarily had associated settlements, where attachment may not have been voluntary or for wholly spiritual reasons. This relationship nevertheless would have influenced the life and spirituality of the area. Apparently some people were enrolled specifically as *confratres* as early as the ninth century. These people gave part or all of their assets to a monastery and offered their obedience in return for a guaranteed pension. This expanded to include persons described as members of the faithful, both poor and rich, who requested association with the monastery. In return, they were considered to share spiritually in the prayer, almsgiving or other good works of the monastery. The community made special prayer for these associates in their lifetimes and after death. Eventually, the word "oblate" came to be identified with such individuals who enter into a permanent relationship with a particular group of monastic men or women.

In the mid-eleventh century, William, abbot of Hirschau (d. 1091), established rules for two types of oblates, those living in a monastery without vows and those living in the world but affiliated with a monastery. By the time of Frances of Rome (1384–1440), also honored as a special patron of oblates, this was apparently a well established practice. She organized a group of women who engaged in prayer and service, incorporating Benedictine spirituality into their lives in association with a local monastery.

By 1590 Abbot Tortorici is said to have gathered what was already in use when he made his rules for the reception of oblates. The life of Elena Piscopia, first woman doctor of philosophy at Padua in the 1600s, also describes some of the aspects of her association with the monastery of which she was an oblate. From these, it is evident that much of the current custom and understanding was already well established hundreds of years ago. The tradition has continued in many forms and places, attracting a vast array of persons. In recent years, there has been a resurgence of popularity of the oblate movement, with some communities having large numbers of persons associated with them, sharing in the prayer and work in various ways.

Not everyone who is touched by the spirit of St. Benedict and his followers will become an oblate. Some will simply want to pray some form of the monastic liturgy of the hours, engage in personal contemplation and strive to lead a life which demonstrates the kinds of virtues which Benedict most revered. However, for those who desire a more formal, permanent commitment, any man or woman can become part of the monastic family of any monastery (of either gender) which accepts oblates. These persons make a formal commitment to Benedictine prayer and values. They are united to the prayers and works of the monastery to which they are oblates, even as they continue to carry on their lives in their own locale and lifestyle. Just as the word "oblate" comes from a root word denoting the offering of a gift, each oblate's life is an offering to God and a gift to the monastery which is enriched by the oblate's presence and prayer.

Judith Sutera, O.S.B.

PRAYING THE LITURGY
OF THE HOURS

The Liturgy of the Hours, or the Divine Office, surrounds the rhythms of the day with prayer. While the monastic tradition provides for several periods of prayer, it is usually most possible for persons to frame the day with two major periods of prayer, morning and evening. A short midday and night prayer are also often added. Although these prayers are ideally said in common with others, they may be adapted for individual use.

The following is a simplified version for personal or group prayer, using a two-week cycle. It is intended as an introduction to the Liturgy of the Hours for those who have not regularly used this prayer form or for those who wish to have a monastic prayer book with all components in a single, continuous-text volume for convenience of use. There are various one or more volume prayer books for those who will want a more complete version. Many monasteries make their own locally produced prayer books available to their oblates or others desiring to be more closely united to their community in prayer.

* * * * * *

CALL TO PRAYER: The Office opens with a call to prayer, usually based on a passage of Scripture. Even before the time of St. Benedict, the spiritual writer John Cassian expounded on the use of the words "God, come to my assistance" as a perfect prayer, appropriate to all circumstances.

ANTIPHONS: Antiphons are short sentences from Scripture or spiritual writings which are said before and after the psalms and canticles. Different antiphons are provided for different seasons of the Church year, reflecting the mood of that season. The Advent/Christmas antiphons are used from the beginning of Advent until the end of the Christmas season (Feast of the Baptism of the Lord). Easter antiphons are used from Easter until the Feast of Pentecost. Ordinary time is any period not in Lent or the above mentioned seasons.

PSALMS: In an abbreviated form of the Hours, such as that provided here, not all 150 psalms can be used. Those who wish may supplement this format by using additional psalms prayed from their Bible or from a complete psalter. The same psalms are used with the various antiphons in the seasons of the liturgical year, except that the word "hallelujah" is omitted when praying the psalm in the season of Lent.

While modern people sometimes tend to think of the spoken words of these psalms as their prayer to God, the early monastics had a broader approach. They saw Scripture as the way in which God communicates, or in which people share their faith history. The communication with God takes place in the meditative silence and listening which surround the words. Therefore, a rhythm of word and silence is most important.

READINGS: Although short readings are provided here for convenience, a broader use of Scripture is encouraged. Whenever available, one might read a chapter or shorter segment from the Bible each day with the Liturgy of the Hours, so that an entire book of Scripture is read from beginning to end over a period of time. This is known as *lectio continua* and is desirable for providing both a greater range of material for meditation and a greater familiarity with lesser known portions of Scripture.

GOSPEL CANTICLE: It has been traditional in monastic prayer to include, along with the psalms of the Old Testament, one of the hymns of praise from the New Testament. For morning, it is the canticle of Zachary at the birth of John the Baptist. In the evening the *Magnificat* of Mary at the Annunciation is used. This unites the world of the Old Testament, expressed in the psalms, with the proclamation of salvation through Jesus Christ expressed in the New Testament.

INTERCESSIONS: Intercessions join praise of God with recognition of the need for God's continued blessing. One should petition God not only for personal desires, but pray also for the needs of others and for contemporary concerns of the church and world.

CLOSING PRAYERS: These prayers draw together all that has gone before and call down God's blessings as one goes forth. St. Benedict reminds that the Lord's Prayer should be a prayer of reconciliation with others as well. The final prayers printed here link the day's prayer to some key concept in Benedictine spirituality. Any spontaneous prayer arising from the psalms, reading, or circumstances of one's life may be used as a closing prayer.

FEASTS AND COMMONS: Special prayers may be used for certain feast days. This book contains special offices for use on feast days of Jesus or Mary. There is also a common office that may be used on the feast days of apostles or martyrs whom the user may wish especially to commemorate. For saints who were not apostles or martyrs, there is a common of holy men and women, which includes special antiphons for the feasts of Benedictine saints.

COMPLINE: Compline is one of the other Hours of liturgical prayer. It is usually said at night before retiring. The repetition of the same short psalms each night makes it possible to memorize and pray in darkness, as was most often the custom in early monastic communities. It is a prayer for the loving protection of God both through the night and at the unknown time of one's death.

* * * * * *

The Liturgy of the Hours is ideally a group prayer. For communal prayer it is customary for the participants to alternate the stanzas of the psalms between two equal groups, between the assembly and a leader, or in some other way. A prayer leader would say the first phrase of the opening call to prayer, to which the assembly would respond, would begin each psalm by saying the first line, and would lead the closing prayers. This text is arranged for either private or group usage.

There are many psalm tone melodies to which the psalms may be chanted rather than recited, or a song based on a psalm might be substituted for the recited version. The addition of opening or closing hymns is also appropriate, as is the inclusion of a Scriptural canticle, which is customarily inserted between the psalms.

Canticles have not been included in this text since this is an abbreviated form, but the following are those which occur in the full Liturgy of the Hours:

Old Testament (usually used with morning prayer)

Exod 15:1-18; Deut 32:1-12; 1 Sam 2:1-10; 1 Chron 29:10-13; Tob 13:1-7; Tob 13:8-11, 13-14; Jud 16:2-3a, 13-15; Prov 9:1-6, 10-12; Wis 3:1-9; Wis 9:1-6, 9-11; Wis 10:17-21; Wis 16:20-21, 26; 17:1a; Sir 14:20; 15:3-5a, 6b; Sir 31:8-11; Sir 36:1-7, 13-22, Sir 39:13-16a; Isa 2:2-5; Isa 9:1-6; Isa 12:1-6; Isa 26:1-4, 7-9, 12; Isa 33:2-10; Isa 33:13-16; Isa 38:10-14, 17-20; Isa 40:10-17; Isa 42:10-16; Isa 45:15-25; Isa 49:7-13; Isa 61:6-9; Isa 61:10–62:7; Isa 63:1-5; Isa 66:10-14a; Jer 7:2-7; Jer 14:17-21; Jer 17:7-8; Jer 31:10-14; Lam 5:1-7, 15-17, 19-21; Ezra 36:24-28; Dan 3:26, 27, 29, 34-41; Dan 3:52-57; Dan 3:56-88; Hos 6:1-6; Hab 3:2-4, 13a, 15-19; Zeph 3:8-13

New Testament (usually used at evening prayer or mornings in the Easter season)

Eph 1:3-10; Phil 2:6-11; Col 1:12-20; 1 Tim 3:16; 1 Pet 2:21-24; Rev 4:11 and 5:9, 10, 12; Rev 11:17-18 and 12:10b-12a; Rev 15:3-4; Rev 19:1-7

Midday prayer has also been omitted from this brief prayer book. One traditional option is to pray a section or two from psalm 119 (118) with a short time of meditation or closing prayer.

Judith Sutera, O.S.B.

PRAYING THE PSALMS

The heart of the Liturgy of the Hours is the praying of the psalms. Psalm prayer is not easy; it takes a bit of getting used to. It is not immediately obvious why Christians should spend the greatest share of their prayer time with songs that were already centuries old at the time of Jesus. These psalms, however, remain the staple of Christian prayer. Why?

The Book of Psalms is a collection of prayers composed and kept by the believing community of ancient Israel. The fact that they are still kept by Jews and Christians alike is testimony to our common belief that God still speaks to us through these prayers. In the psalms there is a powerful joining of God's word to us and our word to God. We read them as God's word to us; we take the gift of that word, fill it with our own life's experience, and return it to God. For Christians there is the added insight that the psalms were the primary prayer of Jesus. He still prays them in and with us today.

The psalms reflect the whole gamut of human existence. The cry of terror, the groan of pain, the sigh of contentment, the gasp of awe are all expressed in the prayer of the psalms. In the laments we complain to God about the fears and tragedies of our lives. We ask God to root out everything which diminishes us. We rage against unjust suffering and violence. We weep over sin. Our prayer itself is violent. It is an acknowledgment of the anger that nests within us. It is also an acknowledgment that, left to ourselves, we would lash out against those who hurt us. Therefore we bring our anger and our frustration to God. We trust God to restore goodness to our lives because we know that we cannot.

After the pain of the laments we move to prayers of thanksgiving. God does deliver us from evil. God does protect us, even from ourselves. The psalms of thanksgiving reflect that fragile moment when the pain stops. As we continue to experience God's salvation, we are able to pray the psalms of confidence. "The Lord is my light and my salvation; there is nothing I shall fear" (Ps 27:1). "The Lord is my shepherd; I shall not want" (Ps 23:1). We call everyone to trust in God. Finally, we become free enough to turn our whole attention to God and sing the hymns, prayers of praise and wonder at God's overwhelming goodness and love.

The psalms are earthy prayers. We have the nerve to urge God to wake up. We complain, "How long, O Lord!" We praise the gifts of wine and bread, of friendship and singing and dancing. We delight in the simple joy of living. There is no moment of life that is not reflected in the psalms.

We cannot forget, however, that these prayers were written thousands of years ago in a language we do not speak, from a culture we do not experience, in a country different from our own. Some of the images are foreign to us. Most of us have no acquaintance with sheep and have no idea of the significance of a rocky fortress. Our belief in resurrection has become so much a part of our world view that we forget that the notion of life after death was only gradually revealed to God's people.

How can we learn to fully appreciate these prayers? First of all, we must be willing to live with them. We must be willing to pray them over and over, even when they do not speak to us. Secondly, it is useful to take a single image or a single phrase and chew it for a day, a week, a month. How does this word relate to the reality of my life? Thirdly, we may not ignore the psalms that we would rather avoid. What catches me in this psalm? Am I reluctant to face the violence in my own life, or the longing, or even to abandon myself to joy? What can I not hear in this prayer? Finally, we will grow to love the psalms. They will begin to illuminate all the corners of our existence. They will begin to nourish us. They will become for us what they truly are: the Word of Life.

Irene Nowell, O.S.B.

WEEK I—SATURDAY
EVENING PRAISE

O God, come to my assistance/ make haste to help me. Glory be to the Father, and to the Son, and to the Holy Spirit. As it was in the beginning, is now, and ever shall be, world without end. Amen.

ANTIPHON

(Ordinary):   In the night, I meditate in my heart.

(Advent/Christmas):   Come, Radiant Dawn, splendor of eternal light, sun of justice.

(Lent):   In your justice, rescue and deliver me.

(Easter):   May those who love your salvation say always, "God be glorified!"

PSALM 146 (145)

Hallelujah!

Praise the Lord, my heart!
My whole life, give praise.
Let me sing to God
as long as I live.

Never depend on rulers:
born of earth, they cannot save.
They die, they turn to dust.
That day, their plans crumble.

They are wise who depend on God,
who look to Jacob's Lord,

creator of heaven and earth,
maker of the teeming sea.

The Lord keeps faith for ever,
giving food to the hungry,
justice to the poor,
freedom to captives.

The Lord opens blind eyes
and straightens the bent,
comforting widows and orphans,
protecting the stranger.
The Lord loves the just
but blocks the path of the wicked.

Zion, praise the Lord!
Your God reigns for ever,
from generation to generation.
Hallelujah!

(silent reflection)

PSALM 67 (66)

Favor and bless us, Lord.
Let your face shine on us,
revealing your way to all peoples,
salvation the world over.

Let the nations sing your praise,
every nation on earth.

The world will shout for joy
for you rule the planet with justice.
In fairness you govern the nations
and guide the peoples of earth.

Let the nations sing your praise,
every nation on earth.

The land delivers its harvest,
God, our God, has blessed us.
O God, continue your blessing,
may the whole world worship you.

Glory be . . . .

(Repeat antiphon)

READING   [2 Pet 3:8-11, 13-15a]

But do not ignore this one fact, beloved, that with the Lord one day is like a thousand years, and a thousand years are like one day. The Lord is not slow about promise, as some think of slowness, but is patient with you, not wanting any to perish, but all to come to repentance. But the day of the Lord will come like a thief, and then the heavens will pass away with a loud noise, and the elements will be dissolved with fire, and the earth and everything that is done on it will be disclosed.

Since all these things are to be dissolved in this way, what sort of persons ought you to be in leading lives of holiness and godliness? But, in accordance with the promise, we wait for new heavens and a new earth, where righteousness is at home.

Therefore, beloved, while you are waiting for these things, strive to be found by God at peace, without spot or blemish; and regard the patience of our Lord as salvation.

(silent reflection)

MAGNIFICAT ANTIPHON

(Ordinary):   **Blest be our God who bears us day by day.**

(Advent/Christmas):   **Come, Emmanuel; save us, our God!**

(Lent):   **God did not reject my plea, but pledged constant love.**

(Easter):   **Let us rejoice then in God, who rules forever with might.**

MAGNIFICAT

I acclaim the greatness of the Lord,
I delight in God my Savior,
who regarded my humble state.
Truly from this day on
all ages will call me blest.

For God, wonderful in power,
has used that strength for me.
Holy the name of the Lord!
whose mercy embraces the faithful,
one generation to the next.

The mighty arm of God
scatters the proud in their conceit,
pulls tyrants from their thrones,
and raises up the humble.
The Lord fills the starving
and lets the rich go hungry.

God rescues lowly Israel,
recalling the promise of mercy,

the promise made to our ancestors,
to Abraham's heirs for ever.

Glory be . . . .

(Repeat Magnificat antiphon)

INTERCESSIONS

Our Father . . . .

Patient God, you await us lovingly even as we
await your coming. Forgive our frequent drifting
by disobedience away from you. Help us daily to
put your words into action and to strive to live in
peace and holiness, through the example of Jesus
and the guidance of your Holy Spirit. Amen.

May God bless us, deliver us from all evil, and
bring us to everlasting life. Amen.

Let us bless God/ and give thanks.

WEEK I—SUNDAY
MORNING PRAISE

O God, open my lips,/ and my mouth will declare
your praise. Glory be . . . .

(Ordinary):   **May all the earth give you worship
and praise, sing to your name, O God Most High.**

(Advent/Christmas):   **I will raise up for David a just
shoot. He will do what is right and just in the land.**

(Lent):   **Let us return to the God who loves us; let
us turn our ears to God's calling.**

(Easter):   **"I am the resurrection and the life."**

PSALM 19 (18)

The sky tells the glory of God,
tells the genius of God's work.
Day carries the news to day,
night brings the message to night,

without a word, without a sound,
without a voice being heard,
and yet their message fills the world,
their news reaches its rim.

There God has pitched a tent
for the sun to rest and rise renewed
like a bridegroom rising from bed,
an athlete eager to run the race.

It springs from the edge of the earth,
runs a course across the sky
to win the race at heaven's end.
Nothing on earth escapes its heat.

God's perfect law
revives the soul.
God's stable rule
guides the simple.

God's just demands
delight the heart.
God's clear commands
sharpen vision.

God's faultless decrees
stand for ever.
God's right judgments
keep their truth.

Their worth is more than gold,
the purest gold;
their taste richer than honey,
sweet from the comb.

Keeping them makes me rich,
they bring me light;
yet faults hide within us,
forgive me mine.

Keep my pride in check,
break its grip;
I shall be free of blame
for deadly sin.

Keep me, thought and word,
in your good grace.

Lord, you are my Savior,
you are my Rock.

(silent reflection)

PSALM 148

Hallelujah!

Praise the Lord!
Across the heavens,
from the heights,
all you angels, heavenly beings,
sing praise, sing praise!

Sun and moon, glittering stars,
sing praise, sing praise.
Highest heavens, rain clouds,
sing praise, sing praise.

Praise God's name,
whose word called you forth
and fixed you in place for ever
by eternal decree.

Let there be praise:
from depths of the earth,
from creatures of the deep.

Fire and hail, snow and mist,
storms, winds,
mountains, hills,
fruit trees and cedars,
wild beasts and tame,
snakes and birds,

princes, judges,
rulers, subjects,
men, women,
old and young,
praise, praise the holy name,
this name beyond all names.

God's splendor above the earth,
above the heavens,
gives strength to the nation,
glory to the faithful,
a people close to the Lord.
Israel, let there be praise!

(silent reflection)

PSALM 150

Hallelujah!

Praise! Praise God in the temple,
in the highest heavens!
Praise! Praise God's mighty deeds
and noble majesty.

Praise! Praise God with trumpet blasts,
with lute and harp.
Praise! Praise God with timbrel and dance,
with strings and pipes.

Praise! Praise God with crashing cymbals,
with ringing cymbals.
All that is alive, praise. Praise the Lord.
Hallelujah!

Glory be . . . .

(Repeat antiphon)

READING   [Dan 3:51-52, 57-58, 88-90]

Then the three with one voice praised and glorified and blessed God in the furnace:

"Blessed are you, O Lord, God of our ancestors,
and to be praised and highly exalted forever;
And blessed is your glorious, holy name,
and to be highly exalted forever. . . .
Bless the Lord, all you works of the Lord;
sing praise to God and highly exalt God forever. . . .
For God has rescued us from Hades and saved us
    from the power of death,
and delivered us from the midst of the burning
    fiery furnace; from the midst of the fire God
    delivered us.
Give thanks to the Lord, for God is good,
for the mercy of God endures forever.
All who worship the Lord, bless the God of gods,
sing praise and give thanks,
for God's mercy endures forever."

(silent reflection)

BENEDICTUS ANTIPHON

(Ordinary):   **We have come to know and believe in the love God has for us.**

(Advent/Christmas):   **I will fulfill the promise I made to the house of Israel and Judah.**

(Lent):   **God, you are good and forgiving, full of love to all who call.**

(Easter):   **Anyone who lives and believes in me will have eternal life.**

BENEDICTUS

Praise the Lord, the God of Israel,
who shepherds the people and sets them free.

God raises from David's house
a child with power to save.
Through the holy prophets
God promised in ages past
to save us from enemy hands,
from the grip of all who hate us.

The Lord favored our ancestors
recalling the sacred covenant,
the pledge to our ancestor Abraham,
to free us from our enemies,
so we might worship without fear
and be holy and just all our days.

And you, child, will be called
Prophet of the Most High,
for you will come to prepare
a pathway for the Lord
by teaching the people salvation
through forgiveness of their sin.

Out of God's deepest mercy
a dawn will come from on high,
light for those shadowed by death,
a guide for our feet on the way to peace.

Glory be . . . .

(Repeat Benedictus antiphon)

INTERCESSIONS

Our Father . . . .

Blessed are you, God of all creation. Let us who are made in your image and are sustained by your hand reflect you in all that we do, that in all things you may be glorified, forever and ever. Amen.

May God bless us and keep us. May God smile upon us and be gracious to us. May God look upon us kindly and give us peace. Amen.

Let us bless God/ and give thanks.

WEEK I—SUNDAY
EVENING PRAISE

O God, come to my assistance,/ make haste to help me. Glory be . . . .

ANTIPHON

(Ordinary):   **Praised are you, O God, in Jesus Christ. In him you have made the glory of your name to dwell among us.**

(Advent/Christmas):   **Let us set ourselves to know God; that God will come is as certain as the dawn.**

(Lent):   **Examine me, God, and try me, O test my heart and my mind.**

(Easter):   **At the name of Jesus every knee must bend, in heaven, on earth, and under the earth.**

PSALM 1

**If you would be happy:
never walk with the wicked,
never stand with sinners,
never sit among cynics,
but delight in the Lord's teaching
and study it night and day.**

**You will stand like a tree
planted by a stream,
bearing fruit in season,
its leaves never fading,
its yield always plenty.**

Not so for the wicked,
like chaff they are blown by the wind.
They will not withstand the judgment,
nor assemble with the just.
The Lord marks the way of the upright,
but the corrupt walk to ruin.

(silent reflection)

PSALM 110 (109)

The Lord decrees to the king:
"Take the throne at my right hand,
I will make your enemies a footrest.
I will raise your scepter
over Zion and beyond,
over all your enemies.

"Your people stand behind you
on the day you take command.
You are made holy, splendid
newborn like the dawn,
fresh as the dew."

God's oath is firm:
"You are a priest for ever,
the rightful king by my decree."
The Lord stands at your side
to destroy kings
on the day of wrath.

God executes judgment,
crushes the heads of nations,
and brings carnage worldwide.

The victor drinks
from a wayside stream
and rises refreshed.

(silent reflection)

PSALM 111 (110)

Hallelujah!

With my whole heart
I praise the Lord among the just.
Great are God's works,
a delight to explore.
In splendor, in majesty,
God's justice will stand.

Who can forget God's wonders,
a God, merciful and kind
who nourished the faithful,
upheld the covenant,
and revealed mighty deeds,
giving them the land of pagans.

Faithful, just, and true
are all God's decrees:
each law in its place,
valid for ever.

The Lord redeems the faithful,
decrees a lasting covenant.
Holy and awesome God's name!

Fear of the Lord is wisdom's crown,
wise are those who live by it.
Praise the Lord for ever!

Glory be . . . .

(Repeat antiphon)

READING   [Gal 3:23-29]

Now before faith came, we were imprisoned and guarded under the law until faith would be revealed. Therefore the law was our disciplinarian until Christ came, so that we might be justified by faith. But now that faith has come, we are no longer subject to a disciplinarian, for in Christ Jesus you are all children of God through faith. As many of you as were baptized into Christ have clothed yourselves with Christ. There is no longer Jew or Greek, there is no longer slave or free, there is no longer male and female; for all of you are one in Christ Jesus. And if you belong to Christ, then you are Abraham's offspring, heirs according to the promise.

(silent reflection)

MAGNIFICAT ANTIPHON

(Ordinary):   **My soul give praise to God. I will praise God all my days.**

(Advent):   **May we know your way upon earth, O God, that we may give witness to you among the nations.**

(Lent):   **In your love, hear my voice, O God. Give me life by your decrees.**

(Easter):   **Just as in Adam all die, so in Christ all will be made alive.**

MAGNIFICAT

I acclaim the greatness of the Lord,
I delight in God my Savior,
who regarded my humble state.
Truly from this day on
all ages will call me blest.

For God, wonderful in power,
has used that strength for me.
Holy the name of the Lord!
whose mercy embraces the faithful,
one generation to the next.

The mighty arm of God
scatters the proud in their conceit,
pulls tyrants from their thrones,
and raises up the humble.
The Lord fills the starving
and lets the rich go hungry.

God rescues lowly Israel,
recalling the promise of mercy,
the promise made to our ancestors,
to Abraham's heirs for ever.

Glory be . . . .

(Repeat Magnificat antiphon)

INTERCESSIONS

Our Father . . . .

Creator of all people, unite us. Help us to put aside
our prejudices, our suspicions, our misunderstand-
ings, and see in one another the Christ who lives in

each of us, as we praise and worship you, Creator, Savior, Spirit. Amen.

May God bless us, deliver us from all evil, and bring us to everlasting life. Amen.

Let us bless God/ and give thanks.

WEEK I—MONDAY
MORNING PRAISE

O God, open my lips,/ and my mouth will declare your praise. Glory be . . . .

ANTIPHON

(Ordinary): **Beloved, live in love as Christ loved us.**

(Advent): **Be careful, then, how you live, not as unwise people but as wise.**

(Lent): **In this time of repentance, we cry out for your mercy.**

(Easter): **Jesus Christ is truly risen, Alleluia, Alleluia!**

PSALM 5

**Hear my words, my groans,
my cries for help,
O God my king.
I pray to you, Lord,
my prayer rises with the sun.
At dawn I plead my case and wait.**

**You never welcome evil, God,
never let it stay.
You hate arrogance
and abhor scoundrels,
you detest violence
and destroy the traitor.**

But by your great mercy
I enter your house
and bend low in awe
within your holy temple.

In the face of my enemies
clear the way,
bring me your justice.

Their charges are groundless,
they breathe destruction;
their tongues are smooth,
their throat an open grave.

God, pronounce them guilty,
catch them in their own plots,
expel them for their sins;
they have betrayed you.

But let those who trust you
be glad and celebrate for ever.
Protect those who love your name,
then they will delight in you.

For you bless the just, O God,
your grace surrounds them like a shield.

(silent reflection)

PSALM 72 (71)

God, give your king judgment,
the son of the king
your sense of what is right;
help him judge your people
and do right for the powerless.

May mountains bear peace,
hills bring forth justice.
May the king defend the poor,
set their children free,
and kill their oppressors.

May he live as long as the sun,
as long as the moon, for ever.
May he be like rain on a field,
like showers that soak the earth.

May justice sprout in his time
peace till the moon is no more.
May he rule from sea to sea,
from the River to the ends of the earth.

Enemies will cower before him,
they will lick the dust.
Kings from Tarshish and the islands
will bring their riches to him.

Kings of Sheba, kings of Saba
will carry gifts to him.
All kings will bow before him,
all the nations serve him.

He will rescue the poor at their call,
those no one speaks for.
Those no one cares for
he hears and will save,
save their lives from violence,
lives precious in his eyes.

Every day they pray for him,
bless him all his life.
Long life to him!
Gold to him from Saba!

May wheat be thick in the fields,
fruit trees sway on the slope.
May cities teem with people,
thick as the forests of Lebanon.

May his name live on for ever,
live as long as the sun.
May all find blessing in him,
and he be blest by all.

Blest be Israel's God,
Lord of wonderful deeds!
Bless God's name for ever!
Let God's glory fill the world!
Amen and Amen!

Glory be . . . .

(Repeat antiphon)

READING   [1 Cor 1:26-31]

Consider your own call, brothers and sisters: not
many of you were wise by human standards, not
many were powerful, not many were of noble birth.
But God chose what is foolish in the world to shame
the wise; God chose what is weak in the world to
shame the strong; God chose what is low and despised
in the world, things that are not, to reduce to nothing
things that are, so that no one might boast in the
presence of God. God is the source of your life in
Christ Jesus, who became for us wisdom from God,
and righteousness and sanctification and redemption,
in order that, as it is written, "Let the one who boasts,
boast in the Lord."

(silent reflection)

BENEDICTUS ANTIPHON

(Ordinary):   **Show me your way, so that I may walk in your truth.**

(Advent/Christmas):   **You will see the Son of Man coming on a cloud of great power and glory.**

(Lent):   **This is the time of fulfillment. Believe in the Good News.**

(Easter):   **This is the day that God has made: let us rejoice and be glad.**

BENEDICTUS

**Praise the Lord, the God of Israel,
who shepherds the people and sets them free.**

**God raises from David's house
a child with power to save.
Through the holy prophets
God promised in ages past
to save us from enemy hands,
from the grip of all who hate us.**

**The Lord favored our ancestors
recalling the sacred covenant,
the pledge to our ancestor Abraham,
to free us from our enemies,
so we might worship without fear
and be holy and just all our days.**

**And you, child, will be called
Prophet of the Most High,
for you will come to prepare
a pathway for the Lord**

by teaching the people salvation
through forgiveness of their sin.

Out of God's deepest mercy
a dawn will come from on high,
light for those shadowed by death,
a guide for our feet on the way to peace.

Glory be . . . .

(Repeat Benedictus antiphon)

INTERCESSIONS

Our Father . . . .

Giver of all gifts, you love and choose us, your least
ones. Increase our humility so that we might rejoice
in the generosity of your love and be mindful that
the good in us comes from you, Creator, Redeemer
and Spirit, now and forever. Amen.

May God bless us and keep us. May God smile
upon us and be gracious to us. May God look upon
us kindly, and give us peace. Amen.

Let us bless God/ and give thanks.

WEEK I—MONDAY
EVENING PRAISE

O God, come to my assistance,/ make haste to help
me. Glory be . . . .

(Ordinary):   Whoever receives me receives God
who sent me.

(Advent/Christmas):   Announce the Good News to the
people, saying: "Behold, God our savior will come."

(Lent):   Bring us back to you and to the life your
Son has won.

(Easter):   Christ, risen from the dead, will die no
more.

PSALM 81 (80)

Shout joy to God,
the God of our strength,
sing to the God of Jacob.

Lift hearts, strike tambourines,
sound lyre and harp.
Blow trumpets at the New Moon,
till the full moon of our feast.

For this is a law for Israel,
the command of Jacob's God,
decreed for the house of Joseph
when we marched from Egypt.

We heard a voice unknown:
"I lifted burdens from your backs,
a blistering load from your hands.

"You cried out in pain
and I rescued you;
robed in thunder,
I answered you.
At the waters of Meribah
I tested you.

"My people, hear my complaint;
Israel, if you would only listen.
You shall have no other gods,
do not bow before them.
I am the Lord your God.
I brought you out of Egypt
and fed your hungry mouths.

"But you would not hear me,
my people rejected me.
So I hardened your hearts,
and you left me out of your plans.
My people, if you would only listen!
Israel, walk in my ways!

"Then I will strike your enemy,
put them all to flight.
With their fate sealed,
my foes will grovel at your feet.
But you, O Israel,
will feast on finest wheat,
will savor pure wild honey."

(silent reflection)

PSALM 114 (113)

Israel marches out of Egypt,
Jacob leaves an alien people.
Judah becomes a holy place,
Israel, God's domain.

The sea pulls back for them,
the Jordan flees in retreat.
Mountains jump like rams,
hills like lambs in fear.

Why shrink back, O sea?
Jordan, why recoil?
Why shudder, mountains, like rams?
Why quiver, hills, like lambs?

Tremble! earth, before the Lord,
before the God of Jacob,
who turns rock to water,
flint to gushing streams.

Glory be . . . .

(Repeat antiphon)

READING   [Prov 2:1-5, 9-11]

My child, if you accept my words
    and treasure up my commandments within you,
making your ear attentive to wisdom
    and inclining your heart to understanding;
if you indeed cry out for insight,
    and raise your voice for understanding;
if you seek it like silver,
    and search for it as for hidden treasures—
then you will understand the fear of the LORD
    and find the knowledge of God.

Then you will understand righteousness and justice
    and equity, every good path;
for wisdom will come into your heart,
    and knowledge will be pleasant to your soul;
prudence will watch over you;
    and understanding will guard you.

(silent reflection)

MAGNIFICAT ANTIPHON

(Ordinary):   **Forever I will sing the goodness of God.**

(Advent/Christmas):   **He emptied himself, being
born in human likeness.**

(Lent):   **We are led through the waters of death to
become a new creation.**

(Easter):   **I am the first and the last, the one who
lives forever.**

MAGNIFICAT

**I acclaim the greatness of the Lord,
I delight in God my Savior,
who regarded my humble state.
Truly from this day on
all ages will call me blest.**

**For God, wonderful in power,
has used that strength for me.
Holy the name of the Lord!
whose mercy embraces the faithful,
one generation to the next.**

The mighty arm of God
scatters the proud in their conceit,
pulls tyrants from their thrones,
and raises up the humble.
The Lord fills the starving
and lets the rich go hungry.

God rescues lowly Israel,
recalling the promise of mercy,
the promise made to our ancestors,
to Abraham's heirs for ever.

Glory be . . . .

(Repeat Magnificat antiphon)

INTERCESSIONS

Our Father . . . .

Eternal Wisdom, your gifts transform life. Help us
to prefer your ways above all else, to long for
understanding of what is right and just, so that our
eyes may be ever more open to your light, you who
reign forever and ever. Amen.

May God bless us, deliver us from all evil, and
bring us to everlasting life. Amen.

Let us bless God/ and give thanks.

WEEK I—TUESDAY
MORNING PRAISE

O God, open my lips,/ and my mouth will declare your praise. Glory be . . . .

Glory be . . . .

A<small>NTIPHON</small>

(Ordinary):   **Guide me in your truth and teach me, for you are God, my savior.**

(Advent/Christmas):   **Behold our God, the ruler of nations will come. Blessed are they who are prepared to meet him.**

(Lent):   **Those who wish to come after me must practice self-denial, take up their cross and follow me.**

(Easter):   **The disciples recognized Jesus in the breaking of the bread.**

PSALM 8

Lord, our God,
the whole world tells
the greatness of your name.
Your glory reaches
beyond the stars.

Even the babble of infants
declares your strength,
your power to halt
the enemy and avenger.

I see your handiwork
in the heavens:
the moon and the stars
you set in place.

What is humankind
that you remember them,
the human race
that you care for them?

You treat them like gods,
dressing them in glory and splendor.
You give them charge of the earth,
laying all at their feet:

cattle and sheep,
wild beasts,
birds of the sky,
fish of the sea,
every swimming creature.

Lord our God,
the whole world tells
the greatness of your name.

(silent reflection)

PSALM 43 (42)

Decide in my favor, God,
plead my case against the hateful,
defend me from liars and thugs.
For you are God my fortress.

Why have you forgotten me?
Why am I bent double
under the weight of enemies?

Send your light and truth.
They will escort me
to the holy mountain
where you make your home.

I will approach the altar of God,
God, my highest joy,
and praise you with the harp,
God, my God.

Why are you sad, my heart?
Why do you grieve?
Wait for the Lord.
I will yet praise God my savior.

Glory be . . . .

(Repeat antiphon)

READING   [2 Cor 1:3-7]

Blessed be the God and Father of our Lord Jesus Christ, the Father of mercies and the God of all consolation, who consoles us in all our affliction, so that we may be able to console those who are in any affliction with the consolation with which we ourselves are consoled by God. For just as the sufferings of Christ are abundant for us, so also our consolation is abundant through Christ. If we are being afflicted, it is for your consolation and salvation; if we are being consoled, it is for your consolation, which you experience when you patiently endure the same sufferings that we are also suffering. Our hope for you is unshaken; for we know that as you share in our sufferings, so also you share in our consolation.

(silent reflection)

BENEDICTUS ANTIPHON

(Ordinary):   **I will rejoice and be glad, because of your kindness, O God.**

(Advent/Christmas):   **All the earth shall see the salvation by our God.**

(Lent):   **I will bless God day after day. I will bless God's name forever.**

(Easter):   **It is good for me to be with Christ and to put my hope in him.**

BENEDICTUS

Praise the Lord, the God of Israel,
who shepherds the people and sets them free.

God raises from David's house
a child with power to save.
Through the holy prophets
God promised in ages past
to save us from enemy hands,
from the grip of all who hate us.

The Lord favored our ancestors
recalling the sacred covenant,
the pledge to our ancestor Abraham,
to free us from our enemies,
so we might worship without fear
and be holy and just all our days.

And you, child, will be called
Prophet of the Most High,
for you will come to prepare
a pathway for the Lord

by teaching the people salvation
through forgiveness of their sin.

Out of God's deepest mercy
a dawn will come from on high,
light for those shadowed by death,
a guide for our feet on the way to peace.

Glory be . . . .

(Repeat Benedictus antiphon)

INTERCESSIONS

Our Father . . . .

O Great Consoler, you are near us in times of trouble.
Give us courage to see your will in everything, that
we may accept suffering as Jesus did, patiently bear
each other's infirmities, and offer comfort to one
another, through the grace of your Holy Spirit.
Amen.

May God bless us and keep us. May God smile
upon us and be gracious to us. May God look upon
us kindly, and give us peace. Amen.

Let us bless God/ and give thanks.

WEEK I—TUESDAY
EVENING PRAISE

**O God, come to my assistance,/ make haste to help
me. Glory be . . . .**

ANTIPHON

(Ordinary): **God, let your love come upon us, the
saving help of your promise.**

(Advent/Christmas): **God will give strength to this
people and bless us with peace.**

(Lent): **God is my help; therefore, I am not disgraced.**

(Easter): **I call you friends, for I have revealed to
you all that I heard from my Father.**

PSALM 130 (129)

**From the depths I call to you,
Lord, hear my cry.
Catch the sound of my voice
raised up, pleading.**

**If you record our sins,
Lord, who could survive?
But because you forgive
we stand in awe.**

**I trust in God's word,
I trust in the Lord.
More than sentries for dawn
I watch for the Lord.**

More than sentries for dawn
let Israel watch.
The Lord will bring mercy
and grant full pardon.
The Lord will free Israel
from all its sins.

(silent reflection)

PSALM 131 (130)

Lord, I am not proud,
holding my head too high,
reaching beyond my grasp.

No, I am calm and tranquil
like a weaned child
resting in its mother's arms:
my whole being at rest.

Let Israel rest in the Lord,
now and for ever.

(silent reflection)

PSALM 133 (132)

How good it is, how wonderful,
wherever people live as one!

It is like sacred oil on the head
flowing down Aaron's beard,
down to the collar of his robe.
It is like the dew of Hermon
running down the mountains of Zion.

There God gives blessing:
life for ever.

Glory be . . . .

(Repeat antiphon)

READING   [Gen 28:12-16]

[Jacob] dreamed that there was a ladder set up on the earth, the top of it reaching to heaven; and the angels of God were ascending and descending on it. And the LORD stood beside him and said, "I am the LORD, the God of Abraham your father and the God of Isaac; the land on which you lie I will give to you and to your offspring; and your offspring shall be like the dust of the earth, and you shall spread abroad to the west and to the east and to the north and to the south; and all the families of the earth shall be blessed in you and in your offspring. Know that I am with you and will keep you wherever you go, and will bring you back to this land; for I will not leave you until I have done what I have promised you." Then Jacob woke from his sleep and said, "Surely the LORD is in this place— and I did not know it!" And he was afraid, and said, "How awesome is this place! This is none other than the house of God and this is the gate of heaven."

(silent reflection)

MAGNIFICAT ANTIPHON

(Ordinary):   **God, let your love be my guide; stay with me all my life.**

(Advent/Christmas):   **Let the peoples praise you, O God. Let all the peoples praise you.**

(Lent):   **My soul obeys your will and loves it dearly.**

(Easter):   **The love of Christ compels us to live not for ourselves, but for him who died and rose for us.**

MAGNIFICAT

I acclaim the greatness of the Lord,
I delight in God my Savior,
who regarded my humble state.
Truly from this day on
all ages will call me blest.

For God, wonderful in power,
has used that strength for me.
Holy the name of the Lord!
whose mercy embraces the faithful,
one generation to the next.

The mighty arm of God
scatters the proud in their conceit,
pulls tyrants from their thrones,
and raises up the humble.
The Lord fills the starving
and lets the rich go hungry.

God rescues lowly Israel,
recalling the promise of mercy,
the promise made to our ancestors,
to Abraham's heirs for ever.

Glory be . . . .

(Repeat Magnificat antiphon)

INTERCESSIONS

Our Father . . . .

Ever present God, you open for us the way to heaven. Keep us mindful that we stand on holy ground, that all we are and all we do are the ladder leading to you. Bless our days with hope in your promise and our nights with the sense of your presence, through your son Jesus and your Holy Spirit. Amen.

May God bless us, deliver us from all evil, and bring us to everlasting life. Amen.

Let us bless God/ and give thanks.

WEEK I—WEDNESDAY
MORNING PRAISE

O God, open my lips,/ and my mouth shall declare your praise. Glory be . . . .

ANTIPHON

(Ordinary):   **Happy are the people chosen as God's own.**

(Advent/Christmas):   **Make ready the way; clear a straight path for our God.**

(Lent):   **My help comes from God, maker of heaven and earth.**

(Easter):   **All the ends of the earth have seen the salvation of our God.**

PSALM 64 (63)

**Hear my troubles, God.
Keep me safe from terror,
guard me from hostile scheming
and the rage of the violent.**

**Enemies sharpen their tongues
and aim bitter words like arrows
to ambush the innocent
with a sudden, brazen shot.**

**They polish their plans,
conceal their traps,
asking, "Who can see them?"**

They hide the evil they plot.
How devious the heart!

God shoots an arrow,
instantly they are struck.
God trips them on their own tongues.
All who see it tremble.

The whole world stands in awe,
they talk of God's work
and ponder its meaning.
The just rejoice
and find refuge in God.
Honest hearts sing praise.

(silent reflection)

PSALM 42 (41)

As a deer craves running water,
I thirst for you, my God;
I thirst for God,
the living God.
When will I see your face?

Tears are my steady diet.
Day and night I hear,
"Where is your God?"

I cry my heart out,
I remember better days:
when I entered the house of God,
I was caught in the joyful sound
of pilgrims giving thanks.

Why are you sad, my heart?
Why do you grieve?

Wait for the Lord.
I will yet praise God my savior.

My heart is sad.
Even from Jordan and Hermon,
from the peak of Mizar,
I remember you.

There the deep roars to deep;
your torrents crash over me.
the love God summoned by day
sustained my praise by night,
my prayer to the living God.

I complain to God,
who I thought was rock:
"Why have you forgotten me?
Why am I bent double
under the weight of enemies?

"Their insults grind me to dust,
Day and night they say,
`Where is your God?'"

Why are you sad my heart?
Why do you grieve?
Wait for the Lord.
I will yet praise God my savior.

Glory be . . . .

(Repeat antiphon)

READING   [Deut 7:6-10a, 11]

You are a people holy to the LORD your God; the LORD
your God has chosen you out of all the peoples on
earth to be God's people, God's treasured possession.

It was not because you were more numerous than any other people that the LORD set heart on you and chose you—for you were the fewest of all peoples. It was because the LORD loved you and kept the oath that was sworn to your ancestors, that the LORD has brought you out with a mighty hand, and redeemed you from the house of slavery, from the hand of Pharaoh king of Egypt. Know therefore that the LORD your God is God, the faithful God who maintains covenant loyalty with those who love God and keep the commandments, to a thousand generations, and who repays in their own person those who reject God. Therefore, observe diligently the commandment—the statutes, and the ordinances—that I am commanding you today.

(silent reflection)

BENEDICTUS ANTIPHON

(Ordinary):   **Praise God who is good. Sing to our God, who is loving.**

(Advent/Christmas):   **God is leading Israel in joy by the light of glory.**

(Lent):   **You will guide me by your counsel, and so you will lead me to glory.**

(Easter):   **Christ, risen from the dead, will die no more.**

BENEDICTUS

Praise the Lord, the God of Israel,
who shepherds the people and sets them free.

God raises from David's house
a child with power to save.
Through the holy prophets
God promised in ages past
to save us from enemy hands,
from the grip of all who hate us.

The Lord favored our ancestors
recalling the sacred covenant,
the pledge to our ancestor Abraham,
to free us from our enemies,
so we might worship without fear
and be holy and just all our days.

And you, child, will be called
Prophet of the Most High,
for you will come to prepare
a pathway for the Lord
by teaching the people salvation
through forgiveness of their sin.

Out of God's deepest mercy
a dawn will come from on high,
light for those shadowed by death,
a guide for our feet on the way to peace.

Glory be . . . .

(Repeat Benedictus antiphon)

INTERCESSIONS

Our Father . . . .

Saving God, you set your heart on us and made us
your own. May we listen with the ear of our hearts

to the many ways in which your Word and your love will be present to us this day. We ask this through Jesus Christ and in the Spirit. Amen.

May God bless us and keep us. May God smile upon us and be gracious to us. May God look upon us kindly, and give us peace. Amen.

Let us bless God/ and give thanks.

WEEK I—WEDNESDAY
EVENING PRAISE

O God, come to my assistance,/ make haste to help me. Glory be . . . .

A<small>NTIPHON</small>

(Ordinary): **Give praise for God's kindness, for the wonderful deeds towards this people.**

(Advent/Christmas): **Announce the Good News to the people saying: "Behold, God our Savior will come."**

(Lent): **Behold, God is my helper, sustaining my life.**

(Easter): **Jesus Christ is the faithful witness, first born from the dead.**

PSALM 107 (106)

**Give thanks to the Lord of goodness,
for God is lasting love.**

**Let those saved by God
tell their story:
how the Lord snatched them
from the oppressor's might,
gathering them from east and west,
from north and south.**

**They wandered through wasteland,
trekked over sands,
finding no city, no home.
Weak from hunger and thirst,
their lives were fading away.**

Then they cried out to God,
who snatched them from danger,
leading them up a straight road
to a place they could settle.

Let them celebrate God's love,
all the wonders revealed to them.
The Lord slaked their thirst
and filled their aching bellies.

There were some confined in darkness,
chained by suffering,
for they rejected God's word,
scorned the plan of the Most High.
Burdened by their misery,
they fell with no one to help.

Then they cried out,
and God snatched them from danger,
shattering their fetters,
banishing the darkness.

Let them celebrate God's love,
all the wonders revealed to them.
The Lord smashed iron bars
and doors of bronze.

(silent reflection)

PSALM 107 (106) continued

Disease struck down others,
for rebelling in their sin.
Sickened by food,
they almost died.

Then they cried out,
and God snatched them from danger,
spoke a word of healing,
and kept them alive.

Let them celebrate God's love,
all the wonders revealed to them.
Let them offer a sacrifice of praise
and tell their story with joy.

Sailors went down to the sea,
traders on merchant ships,
and saw the works of the Lord,
all the wonders of the deep.

At God's command,
a storm whipped up the waves,
high as the rolling clouds,
low as the fathomless depths.
Seafarers trembled,
lurching and reeling like drunks,
helpless without their skills.

Then they cried out,
and God snatched them from danger,
hushing the wind,
stilling the waters.
They rejoiced in the calm
as God brought them to port.

Let them celebrate God's love,
all the wonders revealed to them.
Let the assembly shout "Hallelujah"
and the elders sing praise in the temple.

God turns rivers into sand,
springs to thirsty ground,
rich earth to salt flats,
when evil dwells in a land.

But God turns desert to flowing water,
dry land to fertile valleys,
and gives this place to the hungry
where they build their city.

They sow crops, plant vines,
and gather the harvest.
With God's blessing they prosper;
people and cattle increase.

But if they fail to prosper
and suffer oppression and pain,
God will scorn their leaders
and let them wander in chaos.
But God will lift up the poor,
shepherding them like flocks.

Good hearts, rejoice!
Evil mouths, be shut!
Let the wise listen
and wonder at God's great love.

Glory be . . . .

(Repeat antiphon)

READING   [Phil 3:7-14]

Whatever gains I had, these I have come to regard
as loss because of Christ. More than that, I regard
everything as loss because of the surpassing value of

knowing Christ Jesus my Lord. For his sake I have suffered the loss of all things, and I regard them as rubbish, in order that I may gain Christ and be found in him, not having a righteousness of my own that comes from the law, but one that comes through faith in Christ, the righteousness from God based on faith. I want to know Christ and the power of his resurrection and the sharing of his sufferings by becoming like him in his death, if somehow I may attain the resurrection from the dead.

Not that I have already obtained this or have already reached the goal; but I press on to make it my own, because Christ Jesus has made me his own. Beloved, I do not consider that I have made it my own; but this one thing I do: forgetting what lies behind and straining forward to what lies ahead, I press on toward the goal for the prize of the heavenly call of God in Christ Jesus.

(silent reflection)

MAGNIFICAT ANTIPHON

(Ordinary):   **Glorify God with me. Together let us praise God's name.**

(Advent/Christmas):   **God strengthens our hearts as we await the coming of Jesus.**

(Lent):   **Give God glory and power. Give the glory due God's name.**

(Easter):   **I will praise the name of God in song; I will glorify God with thanksgiving.**

MAGNIFICAT

I acclaim the greatness of the Lord,
I delight in God my Savior,
who regarded my humble state.
Truly from this day on
all ages will call me blest.

For God, wonderful in power,
has used that strength for me.
Holy the name of the Lord!
whose mercy embraces the faithful,
one generation to the next.

The mighty arm of God
scatters the proud in their conceit,
pulls tyrants from their thrones,
and raises up the humble.
The Lord fills the starving
and lets the rich go hungry.

God rescues lowly Israel,
recalling the promise of mercy,
the promise made to our ancestors,
to Abraham's heirs for ever.

Glory be . . . .

(Repeat Magnificat antiphon)

INTERCESSIONS

Our Father . . . .

Great God, the prize towards which we run, focus
our eyes on the power of Christ's resurrection. Let
nothing distract us from our goal and expand our

hearts by love to hasten towards you. We ask this in the power of the Spirit. Amen.

May God bless us, deliver us from all evil and bring us to everlasting life. Amen.

Let us bless God/ and give thanks.

WEEK I—THURSDAY
MORNING PRAISE

O God, open my lips,/ and my mouth will declare your praise. Glory be . . . .

Antiphon

(Ordinary):   **God, we give thanks to your holy name, and glory in praising you.**

(Advent/Christmas):   **You will be named by God forever the Peace of Justice.**

(Lent):   **If you wish to rank first, you must remain the last one of all and the servant of all.**

(Easter):   **If you are raised with Christ, seek the things that are above.**

PSALM 14 (13)

**Fools tell themselves,
"There is no God."
Their actions are corrupt,
none of them does good.**

**The Lord looks down
to see if anyone is wise,
if anyone seeks God.**

**But all have turned away,
all are depraved.
No one does good,
not even one.**

Are these evil-doers mad?
They eat up my people
like so much bread;
they never pray.

They should cringe in fear,
for God sits with the just.
You may mock the poor,
but the Lord keeps them safe.

If only a savior would come from Zion
to restore the people's fortunes!
Then Jacob would sing,
and Israel rejoice.

(silent reflection)

PSALM 90 (89)

You have been our haven, Lord,
from generation to generation.
Before the mountains existed,
before the earth was born,
from age to age you are God.

You return us to dust,
children of earth back to earth.
For in your eyes a thousand years
are like a single day:
they pass with the swiftness of sleep.

You sweep away the years
as sleep passes at dawn,
like grass that springs up in the day
and is withered by evening.

For we perish at your wrath,
your anger strikes terror.
You lay bare our sins
in the piercing light of your presence.
All our days wither beneath your glance,
our lives vanish like a breath.

Our life is a mere seventy years,
eighty with good health,
and all it gives us
is toil and distress;
then the thread breaks
and we are gone.

Who can know the force of your anger?
Your fury matches our fear.
Teach us to make use of our days
and bring wisdom to our hearts.

How long, O Lord, before you return?
Pity your servants,
shine your love on us each dawn,
and gladden all our days.

Balance our past sorrows
with present joys
and let your servants, young and old,
see the splendor of your work.

Let your loveliness shine on us,
and bless the work we do,
bless the work of our hands.

Glory be . . . .

(Repeat antiphon)

READING [1 Cor 12:4-11]

There are varieties of gifts, but the same Spirit; and there are varieties of services, but the same Lord; and there are varieties of activities, but it is the same God who activates all of them in everyone. To each is given the manifestation of the Spirit for the common good. To one is given through the Spirit the utterance of wisdom, and to another the utterance of knowledge according to the same Spirit, to another faith by the same Spirit, to another gifts of healing by the one Spirit, to another the working of miracles, to another prophecy, to another the discernment of spirits, to another various kinds of tongues, to another the interpretation of tongues. All these are activated by one and the same Spirit, who allots to each one individually just as the Spirit chooses.

(silent reflection)

BENEDICTUS ANTIPHON

(Ordinary): We bless and glorify your name, O God, by acknowledging your Son to be the Holy One of God.

(Advent/Christmas): God will come from the holy place, will come to save the people.

(Lent): Be watchful that you may know the will of God.

(Easter): I am the Alpha and the Omega, the one who lives forever.

BENEDICTUS

Praise the Lord, the God of Israel,
who shepherds the people and sets them free.

God raises from David's house
a child with power to save.
Through the holy prophets
God promised in ages past
to save us from enemy hands,
from the grip of all who hate us.

The Lord favored our ancestors
recalling the sacred covenant,
the pledge to our ancestor Abraham,
to free us from our enemies,
so we might worship without fear
and be holy and just all our days.

And you, child, will be called
Prophet of the Most High,
for you will come to prepare
a pathway for the Lord
by teaching the people salvation
through forgiveness of their sin.

Out of God's deepest mercy
a dawn will come from on high,
light for those shadowed by death,
a guide for our feet on the way to peace.

Glory be . . . .

(Repeat Benedictus antiphon)

INTERCESSIONS

Our Father . . . .

Giver of every good gift, your greatness is glimpsed in the wonder and variety of humanity. Enable us to share our talents freely, humbly and generously, and help us to welcome the gifts of others graciously and gratefully. Triune God, receive our prayer. Amen.

May God bless us and keep us. May God smile upon us and be gracious to us. May God look upon us kindly, and give us peace. Amen.

Let us bless God/ and give thanks.

WEEK I—THURSDAY
EVENING PRAISE

O God, come to my assistance,/ make haste to help me. Glory be . . . .

ANTIPHON

(Ordinary): **My mouth will declare your justice, day by day your salvation.**

(Advent/Christmas): **Let the speech of God be awaited like rain; and let our God come down upon us like dew.**

(Lent): **Turn to me with all your heart. I am tender and compassionate.**

(Easter): **There is nothing to fear. Once I was dead but now I live forever and ever.**

PSALM 141 (140)

**Hurry, Lord! I call and call!
Listen! I plead with you.
Let my prayer rise like incense,
my upraised hands,
like an evening sacrifice.**

**Lord, guard my lips,
watch my every word.
Let me never speak evil
or consider hateful deeds,**

let me never join the wicked
to eat their lavish meals.

If the just correct me,
I take their rebuke as kindness,
but the unction of the wicked
will never touch my head.
I pray and pray
against their hateful ways.

Let them be thrown
against a rock of judgment,
then they will know
I spoke the truth.

Then they will say,
"Our bones lie broken upon the ground,
scattered at the grave's edge."

Lord my God, I turn to you,
in you I find safety.
Do not strip me of life.
Do not spring on me
the traps of the wicked.
Let evildoers get tangled
in their own nets,
but let me escape.

(silent reflection)

PSALM 139 (138)

You search me, Lord, and know me.
Wherever I sit or stand,
you read my inmost thoughts;
whenever I walk or rest,
you know where I have been.

Before a word slips from my tongue,
Lord, you know what I will say.
You close in on me,
pressing your hand upon me.
All this overwhelms me—
too much to understand!

Where can I hide from you?
How can I escape your presence?
I scale the heavens, you are there!
I plunge to the depths, you are there!

If I fly toward the dawn,
or settle across the sea,
even there you take hold of me,
your right hand directs me.

If I think night will hide me
and darkness give me cover,
I find darkness is not dark.
For your night shines like day,
darkness and light are one.

You created every part of me,
knitting me in my mother's womb.
For such handiwork, I praise you.
Awesome this great wonder!
I see it so clearly!

You watched every bone
taking shape in secret,
forming in the hidden depths.
You saw my body grow
according to your design.

You recorded all my days
before they ever began.

How deep are your thoughts!
How vast their sum!
like countless grains of sand,
well beyond my grasp.

Lord, destroy the wicked,
save me from killers.
They plot evil schemes;
they blaspheme against you.

How I hate those who hate you!
How I detest those who defy you!
I hate with a deadly hate
these enemies of mine.

Search my heart, probe me, God!
Test and judge my thoughts.
Look! do I follow crooked paths?
Lead me along your ancient way.

Glory be . . . .

(Repeat antiphon)

READING   [Job 11:5-6, 7-9, 13, 15-18]

But oh, that God would speak
    and open lips to you
and would tell you the secrets of wisdom!
    For wisdom is many-sided.
Can you find out the deep things of God?
    Can you find out the limit of the Almighty?
It is higher than heaven—what can you do?
    Deeper than Sheol—what can you know?
Its measure is longer than the earth
    and broader than the sea.

If you direct your heart rightly,
>you will stretch out your hands toward God.
Surely then you will lift up your face without blemish;
>you will be secure, and will not fear.
You will forget your misery;
>you will remember it as waters that have passed
>>away.
And your life will be brighter than the noonday;
>its darkness will be like the morning.
And you will have confidence, because there is hope;
>you will be protected and take your rest in safety.

(silent reflection)

MAGNIFICAT ANTIPHON

(Ordinary):   **In every age we give you thanks, O
God, for the love you have revealed in Jesus.**

(Advent/Christmas):   **Our God will come from
Lebanon with brightness as the light.**

(Lent):   **Happy are they whose sins are taken away,
whose faults are covered.**

(Easter):   **This is the day that God has made: let us
rejoice and be glad.**

MAGNIFICAT

I acclaim the greatness of the Lord,
I delight in God my Savior,
who regarded my humble state.
Truly from this day on
all ages will call me blest.

For God, wonderful in power,
has used that strength for me.

Holy the name of the Lord!
whose mercy embraces the faithful,
one generation to the next.

The mighty arm of God
scatters the proud in their conceit,
pulls tyrants from their thrones,
and raises up the humble.
The Lord fills the starving
and lets the rich go hungry.

God rescues lowly Israel,
recalling the promise of mercy,
the promise made to our ancestors,
to Abraham's heirs for ever.

Glory be . . . .

(Repeat Magnificat antiphon)

INTERCESSIONS

Our Father . . . .

God who holds all in your loving hands, gift us
with true humility that, in knowing how frail and
small we are, we may rejoice even more in the mag-
nitude of your love and the wonders of our own
giftedness. We ask this through Jesus and the
Spirit. Amen.

May God bless us, deliver us from all evil, and
bring us to everlasting life. Amen.

Let us bless God/ and give thanks.

WEEK I—FRIDAY
MORNING PRAISE

O God, open my lips,/ and my mouth shall declare your praise. Glory be . . . .

(Ordinary): **God has been my strength, has saved me because of love.**

(Advent/Christmas): **Let us live justly and piously, looking for the blessed hope and coming of the savior.**

(Lent): **Anyone among you who aspires to greatness must serve the rest.**

(Easter): **The Son of Man will come in the clouds with great power and glory.**

PSALM 51 (50)

**Have mercy, tender God,
forget that I defied you.
Wash away my sin,
cleanse me from my guilt.**

**I know my evil well,
it stares me in the face,
evil done to you alone
before your very eyes.**

**How right your condemnation!
Your verdict clearly just.**

You see me for what I am,
a sinner before my birth.

You love those centered in truth;
teach me your hidden wisdom.
Wash me with fresh water,
wash me bright as snow.

Fill me with happy songs,
let the bones you bruised now dance.
Shut your eyes to my sin,
make my guilt disappear.

Creator, reshape my heart,
God, steady my spirit.
Do not cast me aside
stripped of your holy spirit.

Save me, bring back my joy,
support me, strengthen my will.
Then I will teach your way
and sinners will turn to you.

Help me, stop my tears,
and I will sing your goodness.
Lord, give me words
and I will shout your praise.

When I offer a holocaust,
the gift does not please you.
So I offer my shattered spirit;
a changed heart you welcome.

In your love make Zion lovely,
rebuild the walls of Jerusalem.
Then sacrifice will please you,
young bulls upon your altar.

(silent reflection)

PSALM 76 (75)

God, you are known throughout Judah,
Israel glories in your name.
Your tent is pitched in Salem,
your command post on Zion.
There you break flaming arrows,
shield and sword and war itself!

Majestic and circled with light,
you seize your prey;
stouthearted soldiers
are stripped of their plunder.
Dazed, they cannot lift a hand.
At your battle cry, God of Jacob,
horse and rider are stunned.

You, the one who strikes fear—
who can stand up to your anger!
Your verdict sounds from heaven;
earth reels, then is still,
when you stand as judge
to defend the oppressed.
When you are robed in fury,
even the warlike give you praise.

Now, all you worshipers,
keep your promise to God,
bring gifts to the Holy One
who terrifies princes
and stuns the rulers of earth.

Glory be . . . .

(Repeat antiphon)

READING   [Ezek 36:22-28]

Thus says the Lord GOD: It is not for your sake, O house of Israel, that I am about to act, but for the sake of my holy name, which you have profaned among the nations to which you came. I will sanctify my great name, which has been profaned among the nations, and which you have profaned among them; and the nations shall know that I am the LORD, says the Lord GOD, when through you I display my holiness before their eyes. I will take you from the nations, and gather you from all the countries, and bring you into your own land. I will sprinkle clean water upon you, and you shall be clean from all your uncleannesses, and from all your idols I will cleanse you. A new heart I will give you, and a new spirit I will put within you; and I will remove from your body the heart of stone and give you a heart of flesh. I will put my spirit within you, and make you follow my statutes and be careful to observe my ordinances.

(silent reflection)

BENEDICTUS ANTIPHON

(Ordinary):   I will sing of God's goodness to me. I will sing to the name of the Most High.

(Advent/Christmas):   Rejoice in God who is near.

(Lent):   Guide me in the path of your commands, for there is my delight.

(Easter):   I will praise God at all times, praise always on my lips.

BENEDICTUS

Praise the Lord, the God of Israel,
who shepherds the people and sets them free.

God raises from David's house
a child with power to save.
Through the holy prophets
God promised in ages past
to save us from enemy hands,
from the grip of all who hate us.

The Lord favored our ancestors
recalling the sacred covenant,
the pledge to our ancestor Abraham,
to free us from our enemies,
so we might worship without fear
and be holy and just all our days.

And you, child, will be called
Prophet of the Most High,
for you will come to prepare
a pathway for the Lord
by teaching the people salvation
through forgiveness of their sin.

Out of God's deepest mercy
a dawn will come from on high,
light for those shadowed by death,
a guide for our feet on the way to peace.

Glory be . . . .

(Repeat Benedictus antiphon)

INTERCESSIONS

Our Father . . . .

Source of Mercy, the life and death of your son are our hope of salvation. Pour the refreshing waters of your love over us. Cleanse our hearts, forgive our failings, and renew our zeal for you as we continue in our conversion throughout our lives. We ask this through Christ our Savior and your Holy Spirit. Amen.

May God bless us and keep us. May God smile upon us and be gracious to us. May God look upon us kindly, and give us peace. Amen.

Let us bless God/ and give thanks.

WEEK I—FRIDAY
EVENING PRAISE

O God, come to my assistance,/ make haste to help me. Glory be . . . .

ANTIPHON

(Ordinary): **God is my rock, my salvation, my stronghold; I shall not be disturbed.**

(Advent/Christmas): **God's greatness shall reach to the ends of the earth. God shall be Peace.**

(Lent): **Christ offered himself only once, to take the faults of many on himself.**

(Easter): **We believe and so we speak. The One who raised Jesus from the dead will raise us up with him.**

PSALM 40 (39)

**I waited and waited for God.
At long last God bent down
to hear my complaint,
and pulled me from the grave
out of the swamp,
and gave me a steady stride
on rock-solid ground.**

**God taught me a new song,
a hymn of praise.
Seeing all this,**

many will be moved
to trust in the Lord.

Happy are they who trust in God,
not seduced by idols
nor won over by lies.

You do so many wonders,
you show you care for us,
Lord my God;
you are beyond compare.
Were I to name them all,
no one could keep track.

You did not seek offerings
or ask for sacrifices;
but you drilled ears
for me to hear.

"Yes," I said, "I will come
to live by your written word."
I want to do what pleases you;
your teaching is in my heart.

I celebrate your justice
before all the assembly;
I do not hold back the story.
Lord, you know this is true.

I did not hide in my heart
your acts of rescue;
I boldly declared to all
your truth and care, your faithful love.

Your maternal love
surrounds me, Lord.
Your sure and tender care
protects me always.

PSALM 40 (39) continued

Countless evils surround me,
more than the hairs on my head;
my sins overwhelm me,
so many I can hardly see.
My courage fails me.

Please, Lord, rescue me;
hurry, Lord, help me.
Stop my killers, shame them,
wipe out my bitter enemies.

Let those who jeer at me,
"Too bad for you!"
be rewarded with shame.

But let all who seek you
and count on your strength
sing and dance and cheer
"Glory to God!"

Though I am weak and poor,
God cares for me.
My help, my savior,
my God, act now!

Glory be . . . .

(Repeat antiphon)

READING   [Acts 10:34-36, 39b-44]

Then Peter began to speak to them: "I truly understand that God shows no partiality, but in every nation anyone who fears God and does what is right is acceptable to God. You know the message sent to the people of Israel, preaching peace by Jesus Christ—he is Lord of all. They put him to death by hanging him on a tree; but God raised him on the third day and allowed him to appear, not to all the people but to us who were chosen by God as witnesses, and who ate and drank with him after he rose from the dead. He commanded us to preach to the people and to testify that he is the one ordained by God as judge of the living and the dead. All the prophets testify about him that everyone who believes in him receives forgiveness of sins through his name."

(silent reflection)

MAGNIFICAT ANTIPHON

(Ordinary):   **Your goodness is greater than life itself; my lips shall ever sing your praise.**

(Advent/Christmas):   **Blessed are they who trust that God's words will be fulfilled.**

(Lent):   **My soul is waiting on God. I count on God's word.**

(Easter):   **Worthy is the Lamb that was slain to receive honor, glory and praise.**

MAGNIFICAT

I acclaim the greatness of the Lord,
I delight in God my Savior,
who regarded my humble state.
Truly from this day on
all ages will call me blest.

For God, wonderful in power,
has used that strength for me.

Holy the name of the Lord!
whose mercy embraces the faithful,
one generation to the next.

The mighty arm of God
scatters the proud in their conceit,
pulls tyrants from their thrones,
and raises up the humble.
The Lord fills the starving
and lets the rich go hungry.

God rescues lowly Israel,
recalling the promise of mercy,
the promise made to our ancestors,
to Abraham's heirs for ever.

Glory be . . . .

(Repeat Magnificat antiphon)

INTERCESSIONS

Our Father . . . .

Just God, the death and resurrection of Jesus are
your great gift to us. As we are mindful of our sins,
keeping death and judgment ever before our eyes,
comfort us also with the hope of your mercy and
the resurrection to which we look forward with joy
and longing, through your Son and Spirit. Amen.

May God bless us, deliver us from all evil, and
bring us to everlasting life. Amen.

Let us bless God/ and give thanks.

WEEK I—SATURDAY
MORNING PRAISE

O God, open my lips,/ and my mouth shall declare your praise. Glory be . . . .

ANTIPHON

(Ordinary): **The time is fulfilled; the Kingdom of God is at hand.**

(Advent/Christmas): **Fear not, be not discouraged. Your God is in your midst.**

(Lent): **Return to me with all your heart, with fasting, weeping and mourning.**

(Easter): **Christ risen from the dead will die no more.**

PSALM 122 (121)

**With joy I heard them say,
"Let us go to the Lord's house!"
And now, Jerusalem,
we stand inside your gates.**

**Jerusalem, the city so built
that city and temple are one.
To you the tribes go up,
every tribe of the Lord.**

**It is the law of Israel
to honor God's name.
The seats of law are here,
the thrones of David's line.**

Pray peace for Jerusalem:
happiness for your homes,
safety inside your walls,
peace in your great houses.

For love of family and friends
I say, "Peace be with you!"
For love of the Lord's own house
I pray for your good.

PSALM 143 (142)

Hear me, faithful Lord!
bend to my prayer,
show compassion.
Do not judge harshly;
in your sight, no one is just.

My enemy hunts me down,
grinding me to dust,
caging me with the dead
in lasting darkness.
My strength drains away,
my heart is numb.

I remember the ancient days,
I recall your wonders,
the work of your hands.
Dry as thirsty land,
I reach out for you.

Answer me quickly, Lord.
My strength is spent.
Do not hide from me
or I will fall into the grave.

Let morning announce your love,
for it is you I trust.
Show me the right way,
I offer you myself.

Rescue me from my foes,
you are my only refuge, Lord.
Teach me your will,
for you are my God.

Graciously lead me, Lord,
on to level ground.
I call on your just name,
keep me safe, free from danger.

In your great love for me,
disarm my enemies
destroy their power,
for I belong to you.

Glory be . . . .

(Repeat antiphon)

READING   [Isa 41:8-13]

You, Israel, my servant,
    Jacob, whom I have chosen,
    the offspring of Abraham, my friend;
you whom I took from the ends of the earth,
    and called from its farthest corners,
saying to you, "You are my servant.
    I have chosen you and not cast you off";
do not fear, for I am with you,
    do not be afraid for I am your God;
I will strengthen you, I will help you,
    I will uphold you with my victorious right hand.

Yes, all who are incensed against you
   shall be ashamed and disgraced;
those who strive against you
   shall be as nothing and shall perish.
You shall seek those who contend with you,
   but you shall not find them;
those who war against you
   shall be as nothing at all.
For I, the LORD your God,
   hold your right hand;
it is I who say to you, "Do not fear,
   I will help you."

(silent reflection)

BENEDICTUS ANTIPHON

(Ordinary):   **God remembers the covenant forever.**

(Advent/Christmas):   **God will rejoice over you in gladness, will renew you in love.**

(Lent):   **Now is the acceptable time. This is the day of salvation.**

(Easter):   **We preach Christ crucified, alleluia. He is the power and the wisdom of God, alleluia.**

BENEDICTUS

Praise the Lord, the God of Israel,
who shepherds the people and sets them free.

God raises from David's house
a child with power to save.
Through the holy prophets
God promised in ages past

to save us from enemy hands,
from the grip of all who hate us.

The Lord favored our ancestors
recalling the sacred covenant,
the pledge to our ancestor Abraham,
to free us from our enemies,
so we might worship without fear
and be holy and just all our days.

And you, child, will be called
Prophet of the Most High,
for you will come to prepare
a pathway for the Lord
by teaching the people salvation
through forgiveness of their sin.

Out of God's deepest mercy
a dawn will come from on high,
light for those shadowed by death,
a guide for our feet on the way to peace.

Glory be . . . .

(Repeat Benedictus antiphon)

INTERCESSIONS

Our Father . . . .

Mighty and tender God who holds us by the hand,
cast out our fears by your love. Help us to love our
enemies, to accept our hardships and to cling firmly
to you, for you have power over all, in the triumph
of Jesus and the presence of the Holy Spirit, one
God forever and ever. Amen.

May God bless us and keep us. May God smile upon us and be gracious to us. May God look upon us kindly, and give us peace. Amen.

Let us bless God/ and give thanks.

THE PRACTICE OF *LECTIO*

One's private time of listening to the Word of God is as important to the Benedictine way of prayer as the praying of the Liturgy of the Hours. This practice is called *lectio*, but the English translation "sacred reading" is inadequate to express the act and its intent.

It is the time which one spends in personal interaction with God's Word. It is not merely reading Scripture or spiritual books. It is not a structured style of meditation or imaging; there is no single "method" for it. Rather, it is making time and space each day to be with the sacred. A word or passage may speak to the praying person, moving from image to image, flowing from thought to feeling. It may set a mood for the day or bring the calming that takes one into the night. It is the transforming presence of God which gradually occupies the space of other thoughts and concerns in one's heart and brings them into oneness with it.

Although Scripture is the primary source for lectio, one may find inspiration in a variety of other readings. Below are some short quotations from the Rule of St. Benedict. Many complete translations of the Rule are divided and dated so one might read a short segment each day.

Judith Sutera, O.S.B.

THOUGHTS FROM THE RULE
OF ST. BENEDICT*

First of all, every time you begin a good work, you must pray to God most earnestly to bring it to perfection. *(Prol 4)*

Let us open our eyes to the light that comes from God, and our ears to the voice from heaven that every day calls out this charge: "If you hear his voice today, do not harden your hearts" [Ps 95]. *(Prol 9)*

Seeking his worker in a multitude of people, the Lord calls out to that one and lifts his voice again: "Is there anyone here who yearns for life and desires to see good days?" [Ps 34] If you hear this and your answer is "I do," God then directs these words to you: If you desire true and eternal life, "keep your tongue free from vicious talk and your lips from all deceit; turn away from evil and do good; let peace be your quest and aim" [Ps 34].

Once you have done this, my "eyes will be upon you and my ears will listen for your prayers; and even before you ask me, I will say to you: Here I am" [Isa 58]. What is more delightful than this voice of the Lord calling to us? See how the Lord in his love shows us the way of life. Clothed then with faith and the performance of good works, let us set out on this way, with the Gospel for our guide, that we may deserve to see him who has called us to his kingdom [1 Thess 2]. *(Prol 14–21)*

These people fear the Lord, and do not become elated over their good deeds; they judge it is the Lord's power, not their own, that brings about the good in them. *(Prol 29)*

Do not be daunted immediately by fear and run away from the road that leads to salvation. It is bound to be narrow at the outset. But as we progress in this way of life and in faith, we shall run on the path of God's commandments, our hearts overflowing with the inexpressible delight of love. *(Prol 48–49)*

Your way of acting should be different than the world's way; the love of Christ should come before all else. *(RB 4:20)*

Rid your heart of all deceit. Never give a hollow greeting of peace or turn away when someone needs your love. *(RB 4:24-26)*

Place your hope in God alone. *(RB 4:41)*

Do not aspire to be called holy before you really are, but first be holy that you may more truly be called so. *(RB 4:62)*

Pray for your enemies out of love for Christ. If you have a dispute with someone, make peace with that one before the sun goes down. *(RB 4:72-73)*

This very obedience, however, will be acceptable to God and agreeable to others only if compliance with what is commanded is not cringing or half-hearted, but free from any grumbling or any reaction of unwillingness. *(RB 5:14)*

Now the ladder erected is our life on earth, and if we humble our hearts the Lord will raise it to heaven. We may call our body and soul the sides of this ladder into which our divine vocation has fitted the various steps of humility and discipline as we ascend. *(RB 7:8-9)*

Through this love, all that they once performed with dread, they will now begin to observe without effort, as though naturally, from habit, no longer out of fear of hell, but out of love for Christ, good habit and delight in virtue. *(RB 7:68-69)*

Let us stand to sing the psalms in such a way that our minds are in harmony with our voices. *(RB 19:7)*

They will regard all utensils and goods of the monastery as sacred vessels of the altar, aware that nothing is to be neglected. *(RB 31:10)*

Whoever needs less should thank God and not be distressed, but whoever needs more should feel humble because of weakness, not self-important because of the kindness shown. In this way all the members will be at peace. *(RB 34:3-5)*

Yet, all things are to be done with moderation on account of the fainthearted. *(RB 48:9)*

All guests who present themselves are to be welcomed as Christ, for he himself will say: "I was a stranger and you welcomed me" [Matt 25]. *(RB 53:1)*

Great care and concern are to be shown in receiving poor people and pilgrims, because in them more particularly Christ is received; our very awe of the rich guarantees them special respect. *(RB 53:15)*

What page, what passage of the inspired books of the Old and New Testaments is not the truest of guides for human life? *(RB 73:3)*

Just as there is a wicked zeal of bitterness which separates from God and leads to hell, so there is a good zeal which separates from evil and leads to God and everlasting life. *(RB 72:1-2)*

"They should each try to be the first to show respect to the other" [Rom 12], supporting with the greatest patience one another's weaknesses of body or behavior, and earnestly competing in obedience to one another. *(RB 72:4-6)*

Let them prefer nothing whatever to Christ, and may he bring us all together to everlasting life. *(RB 72:11-12)*

RB 1980: The Rule of St. Benedict (Collegeville: The Liturgical Press, 1981).

SOME BENEDICTINE PRAYERS

PRAYER FOR A HAPPY DEATH

O holy father, Benedict, blessed by God both in grace and in name, who, while standing in prayer, with your hands raised to heaven, did most happily yield your angelic spirit into the hands of your creator, and have promised zealously to defend against all the snares of the enemy in the last struggle of death, those who shall daily remind you of your glorious departure and your heavenly joys; protect me, I beseech you, O glorious father, this day and every day, by your holy blessing, that I may never be separated from our dear Lord, from the society of yourself, and of all the blessed. Through the same Christ our Lord. Amen.

(Traditional)

PRAYER OF THE CHURCH

Raise up, O Lord, in your church, the spirit wherewith our holy father Benedict the abbot was animated, that filled with the same spirit, we may learn to love what he loved and to practice what he taught. Through Jesus Christ our Lord. Amen.

Grant, we beseech you, O Lord, perseverance in your holy service, and that the people serving you in our days may increase both in spirit and in number. Through Christ our Lord. Amen.

(Traditional)

PRAYER FOR MONASTIC LIFE

O loving God,
we ask your blessing
on all monastic men and women
who live and work
in the most destitute parts of the world.

Help them to become people of prayer and peace.
May they be visible signs
that strangers can live together in God's love.
Give them hearts wide enough
to welcome the traveler, the outcast, the neighbor.
Enable them
to listen to and learn from the people they serve,
especially the poorest.
May their communities be models of wise
   stewardship,
of dignified human labor,
of sacred leisure,
and of reverence for all living things.

Above all, O God,
may a monastic presence in the world
be a constant witness
of justice, compassion and hope to all. Amen.

(Alliance for International Monasticism)

PRAYER FOR PEACE

St. Benedict, you were a man of peace. You walked
the paths of peace your whole life long and led all
who came to you into the ways of peace. Help us,
St. Benedict, to achieve peace: peace in our hearts,

peace in our homes, peace in our sorely troubled world. Through your powerful intercession with God help us to be peacemakers. Aid us to work for peace, to take the first step in ending bitterness, to be the first to hold out our hands in friendship and forgiveness. Beg God to let peace permeate our lives so that they may be lived in God's grace and love. And at the end of our lives obtain for us the reward of the peacemakers, the eternal blessed vision of God in heaven. Amen.

PRAYER FOR A HOLY LIFE

Lord, you chose St. Benedict to follow you and made him the founder of a great religious family in your church. Help me, through his intercession, to choose the vocation you have destined for me and to follow it with generosity, steadfastness and courage all the days of my life. May the spirit of St. Benedict inspire me to prefer nothing to you, to lead a life of prayer, to form myself on your word and to labor for the salvation of all people. I ask this of you, Lord Jesus, who lives and reigns with the Father and the Holy Spirit forever. Amen.

ANNUAL RENEWAL OF OBLATION

Those who have made a permanent commitment as oblates of a monastic community should renew their commitment annually. Ideally, this is done at the monastery or at some gathering of oblates. However, if this is not possible, they may make their renewal privately on the anniversary of their oblation, or on a Benedictine feast day or some other significant date.

I renew my oblation as an Oblate of St. Benedict for the community of (n.), and promise again to serve God and all people according to the Rule of St. Benedict.

Let us pray.

God, most compassionate and loving, strengthen me in my commitment to follow you in the way of St. Benedict. Through my daily prayer and work may I be inspired to live in Christ and to bring his love to the world and his peace to all hearts. I make this prayer through Christ our Lord. Amen.

THE MEDAL AND THE CROSS
OF ST. BENEDICT

Devotion to the cross and to St. Benedict were always cherished in the Benedictine order, and medals of St. Benedict under one type or another were known already in the beginning of the Middle Ages. A manuscript dating back to the year 1415, discovered at the abbey in Metten, Bavaria, in the seventeenth century, gave an explanation of the letters on the medal. This manuscript contained a drawing representing St. Benedict with the cross in one hand and a sort of banner or scroll in the other. The discovery of the sketch and its verses was for the faithful a new incentive to a greater devotion to the holy cross, as well as to St. Benedict. Medals, as symbols of this two-fold devotion, were then struck and distributed among the people.

At present, there are two types of medals. The first is found in various shapes and is known as the "Ordinary Medal." The second, known as the "Jubilee" or "Centenary Medal," was struck in 1880 to commemorate the 1400th anniversary of the birth of St. Benedict and has become the most common design.

The Jubilee Medal of St. Benedict represents on the one side the holy patriarch holding in one hand the cross and in the other the Holy Rule. On the other side is shown a cross with certain letters on and around it. The letters in the angles of the cross, C. S. P. B., stand for the words *Crux Sancti Patris Benedicti* (Cross of Holy Father Benedict).

On the perpendicular bar of the cross are the letters C. S. S. M. L. They signify *Crux Sacra Sit Mihi Lux* (May the holy cross be my light). On the horizontal bar is found N. D. S. M. D. for *Non Draco Sit Mihi Dux* (Let not the Dragon be my guide). Around the margin may be seen V. R. S. N. S. M. V. S. M. Q. L. I. V. B. These initials stand for the verses: *Vade Retro Satana! Nunquam Suade Mihi Vana. Sunt Mala Quae Libas; Ipse Venena Bibas.* (Begone, Satan! Suggest not to me your vain things. The cup you offer me is evil; drink your poison yourself). These or similar words may have been used by St. Benedict when making use of the sign of the cross against the devil and temptations.

Above the cross is the word *PAX* (Peace), the motto of the Benedictine order, to denote a blessing which the medal brings upon the devout wearer. On the other side of the medal is St. Benedict. On his right side is the poisoned cup, shattered by the sign of the cross which the saint made over it. On his left is a raven about to carry away a poisoned loaf of bread sent to him. Above the cup and the raven stands the inscription: *Crux S. Patris Benedicti* (the Cross of Holy Father Benedict). Around the edge of the same side are the words: *Ejus in obitu nostro praesentia muniamur* (At our death may we be protected by his presence). Below is written *Ex S. Monte Casino, MDCCCLXXX* (Abbey of Monte Cassino, 1880).

No special way of carrying or applying the medal is prescribed. No particular prayers are prescribed, as the devout wearing itself is a continual silent prayer. It is the only medal in existence the blessing of which has a special exorcism in the Roman Ritual.

WEEK II—SATURDAY
EVENING PRAISE

O God, come to my assistance,/ make haste to help me. Glory be . . . .

ANTIPHON

(Ordinary):   **Take courage and be stouthearted, all you who hope in God.**

(Advent/Christmas):   **Raise your heads high; your redemption is at hand.**

(Lent):   **I will put my law within you and write it on your hearts.**

(Easter):   **All who were destined for life everlasting believed in the Word of God, alleluia.**

PSALM 20 (19)

God defend you in battle!
Set you safe above the fray!
The God of Jacob send you help,
and from holy Zion, keep you strong!

May God recall your many gifts
and be pleased with your sacrifice,
favoring all your hopes,
making your plans succeed.

Then we will sing of your conquest,
raise the flags in triumph,
to proclaim the name of our God
who grants all you ask.

Now I know for certain:
the anointed of the Lord
is given victory.
God favors him from highest heaven
with a strong, saving hand.

Some boast of chariots and horses,
but we boast of God's name.
They waver and fall,
but we stand firm.

Lord, give victory to your king,
answer us on the day we call.

(silent reflection)

PSALM 147

Hallelujah!

How good to sing God praise!
How lovely the sound!
The Lord rebuilds Jerusalem
and gathers the exiles of Israel,
healing the brokenhearted,
binding their aching wounds.

God fixes the number of stars,
calling each by name.
Great is our God and powerful,
wise beyond all telling.
The Lord upholds the poor
but lets the wicked fall.

Sing thanks to the Lord,
sound the harp for our God.
The Lord stretches the clouds,

sending rain to the earth,
clothing mountains with green.

The Lord feeds the cattle
and young ravens when they call.
A horse's strength, a runner's speed—
they count for nothing!
The Lord favors the reverent,
those who trust in God's mercy.

Jerusalem, give glory!
Praise God with song, O Zion!
For the Lord strengthens your gates
guarding your children within.
The Lord fills your land with peace,
giving you golden wheat.

God speaks to the earth,
the word speeds forth.
The Lord sends heavy snow
and scatters frost like ashes.

The Lord hurls chunks of hail.
Who can stand such cold?
God speaks, the ice melts;
God breathes, the streams flow.

God speaks his word to Jacob,
for Israel, his laws and decrees.
God has not done this for others,
no others receive this wisdom.

Hallelujah!

Glory be . . . .

(Repeat antiphon)

READING   [Rev 21:1-6]

Then I saw a new heaven and a new earth; for the first heaven and the first earth had passed away, and the sea was no more. And I saw the holy city, the new Jerusalem, coming down out of heaven from God, prepared as a bride adorned for her husband. And I heard a loud voice from the throne saying,

"See, the home of God is among mortals.
He will dwell with them as their God;
they will be his peoples,
and God himself will be with them;
he will wipe every tear from their eyes.
Death will be no more;
mourning and crying and pain will be no more,
for the first things have passed away."

And the one who was seated on the throne said, "See, I am making all things new." Also he said, "Write this, for these words are trustworthy and true." Then he said to me, "It is done! I am the Alpha and the Omega, the beginning and the end. To the thirsty I will give water as a gift from the spring of the water of life."

(silent reflection)

MAGNIFICAT ANTIPHON

(Ordinary):   **Steadfast is God's kindness toward us; the fidelity of God endures forever.**

(Advent/Christmas):   **God has made known salvation.**

(Lent):   **You will live in my love if you keep my commandments.**

(Easter):   **Eternal life is this: to know you, the only true God, and the one whom you have sent, Jesus Christ.**

MAGNIFICAT

I acclaim the greatness of the Lord,
I delight in God my Savior,
who regarded my humble state.
Truly from this day on
all ages will call me blest.

For God, wonderful in power,
has used that strength for me.
Holy the name of the Lord!
whose mercy embraces the faithful,
one generation to the next.

The mighty arm of God
scatters the proud in their conceit,
pulls tyrants from their thrones,
and raises up the humble.
The Lord fills the starving
and lets the rich go hungry.

God rescues lowly Israel,
recalling the promise of mercy,
the promise made to our ancestors,
to Abraham's heirs for ever.

Glory be . . . .

(Repeat Magnificat antiphon)

INTERCESSIONS

Our Father . . . .

Alpha and Omega, your reign among us has begun. Let our life here be a reflection of your glorious kingdom and bring us all together to everlasting life with you, Creator, Savior and Spirit. Amen.

May God bless us, deliver us from all evil, and bring us to everlasting life. Amen.

Let us bless God/ and give thanks.

WEEK II—SUNDAY
MORNING PRAISE

O God, open my lips,/ and my mouth shall declare your praise. Glory be . . . .

ANTIPHON

(Ordinary):   **God chose us before the world began to be holy and blameless.**

(Advent/Christmas):   **Behold, the fullness of time has come in which God has sent the Son to the earth.**

(Lent):   **The sufferings of the present are as nothing compared with the glory to be revealed.**

(Easter):   **Christ is risen and makes all things new. He has shown pity to all, alleluia.**

PSALM 46 (45)

**Our sure defense,
our shelter and help in trouble,
God never stands far off.**

**So we stand unshaken
when solid earth cracks
and volcanoes slide into the sea,
when breakers rage
and mountains tremble in the swell.**

**The Lord of cosmic power,
Jacob's God, will shield us.**

A river delights the city of God,
home of the Holy One Most High.
With God there, the city stands.
God defends it under attack.
Nations rage, empires fall.
God speaks, earth melts.

The Lord of cosmic power,
Jacob's God, will shield us.

Come! See the wonders
God does across the earth:
everywhere stopping wars,
smashing, crushing, burning
all the weapons of war.

An end of your fighting!
Acknowledge me as God,
high over nations, high over earth.

The Lord of cosmic power,
Jacob's God, will shield us.

(silent reflection)

PSALM 63 (62)

God, my God, you I crave;
my soul thirsts for you,
my body aches for you
like a dry and weary land.
Let me gaze on you in your temple:
a vision of strength and glory.

Your love is better than life,
my speech is full of praise.
I give you a lifetime of worship,

my hands raised in your name.
I feast at a rich table,
my lips sing of your glory.

On my bed I lie awake,
your memory fills the night.
You have been my help,
I rejoice beneath your wings.
Yes, I cling to you,
your right hand holds me fast.

Let those who want me dead
end up deep in the grave!
They will die by the sword,
their bodies food for jackals.
But let the king find joy in God.
All who swear the truth be praised,
every lying mouth be shut.

(silent reflection)

PSALM 149

Sing a new song, you faithful,
praise God in the assembly.
Israel, rejoice in your maker,
Zion, in your king.
Dance in the Lord's name,
sounding harp and tambourine.

The Lord delights
in saving a helpless people.
Revel in God's glory,
join in clan by clan.
Shout praise from your throat,
sword flashing in hand

to discipline nations
and punish the wicked,
to shackle their kings
and chain their leaders,
and execute God's sentence.
You faithful, this is your glory.

Hallelujah!

Glory be . . . .

(Repeat antiphon)

READING [Rom 8:35-39]

Who will separate us from the love of Christ? Will hardship, or distress, or persecution, or famine, or nakedness, or peril, or sword? As it is written,

> **"For your sake we are being killed all day long; we are accounted as sheep to be slaughtered."**

No, in all these things we are more than conquerors through him who loved us. For I am convinced that neither death, nor life, nor angels, nor rulers, nor things present, nor things to come, nor powers, nor height, nor depth, nor anything else in all creation, will be able to separate us from the love of God in Christ Jesus our Lord.

(silent reflection)

BENEDICTUS ANTIPHON

(Ordinary): **Your will is wonderful indeed; therefore, I obey it.**

(Advent/Christmas): **You heavens, drop down dew from above, and let the clouds rain the just one.**

(Lent): **This is my Son, my Beloved. Listen to him.**

(Easter): **Now is the Son of Man glorified and God is glorified in him.**

BENEDICTUS

**Praise the Lord, the God of Israel,
who shepherds the people and sets them free.**

**God raises from David's house
a child with power to save.
Through the holy prophets
God promised in ages past
to save us from enemy hands,
from the grip of all who hate us.**

**The Lord favored our ancestors
recalling the sacred covenant,
the pledge to our ancestor Abraham,
to free us from our enemies,
so we might worship without fear
and be holy and just all our days.**

**And you, child, will be called
Prophet of the Most High,
for you will come to prepare
a pathway for the Lord
by teaching the people salvation
through forgiveness of their sin.**

**Out of God's deepest mercy
a dawn will come from on high,**

light for those shadowed by death,
a guide for our feet on the way to peace.

Glory be . . . .

(Repeat Benedictus antiphon)

INTERCESSIONS

Our Father . . . .

You are with us, faithful God, revealing yourself in every experience of our lives. Help us to stand firm against all that would take us from you and to rejoice in steadfast perseverance, preferring nothing to your love. We ask this inspired by the life of Jesus and strengthened by the gifts of the Holy Spirit, one God forever. Amen.

May God bless us and keep us. May God smile upon us and be gracious to us. May God look upon us kindly, and give us peace. Amen.

Let us bless God/ and give thanks.

WEEK II—SUNDAY
EVENING PRAISE

**O God, come to my assistance,/ make haste to help
me. Glory be . . . .**

ANTIPHON

(Ordinary):   **Sing a new song to God. Sing, all the
earth.**

(Advent/Christmas):   **Through the tender compassion
of our God, the dawn from on high will break
upon us.**

(Lent):   **My heart has prompted me to seek your
face; do not hide from me.**

(Easter):   **I will not leave you orphans. I will come
back to you and your hearts will rejoice.**

PSALM 95 (94)

**Come, sing with joy to God,
shout to our savior, our rock.
Enter God's presence with praise,
enter with shouting and song.**

**A great God is the Lord,
over the gods like a king.
God cradles the depths of the earth,
holds fast the mountain peaks.
God shaped the ocean and owns it,
formed the earth by hand.**

Come, bow down and worship,
kneel to the Lord our maker.
This is our God, our shepherd;
we are the flock led with care.

Listen today to God's voice:
"Harden no heart as at Meribah,
on that day in the desert at Massah.
There your people tried me,
though they had seen my work.

"Forty years with that lot!
I said: They are perverse,
they do not accept my ways.
So I swore in my anger:
They shall not enter my rest."

(silent reflection)

PSALM 112 (111)

Hallelujah!

Happy those who love God
and delight in the law.
Their children shall be blest,
strong and upright in the land.

Their households thrive,
their integrity stands firm.
A light shines on them in darkness,
a God of mercy and justice.

The good lend freely
and deal fairly,
they will never stumble;
their justice shall be remembered.

Bad news holds no power,
strong hearts trust God.
Steady and fearless,
they look down on their enemy.

They support the poor,
their integrity stands firm.
Their strength brings them honor.

Hatred devours the wicked.
They grind their teeth;
their hopes turn to ashes.

(silent reflection)

PSALM 113 (112)

Hallelujah!

Servants of God, praise,
praise the name of the Lord.
Bless the Lord's name
now and always.
Praise the Lord's name
here and in every place,
from east to west.

The Lord towers above nations,
God's glory shines over the heavens.
Who compares to our God?
Who is enthroned so high?

The Lord bends down
to see heaven and earth,
to raise the weak from the dust
and lift the poor from the mire,

to seat them with princes
in the company of their leaders.

The childless, no longer alone,
rejoice now in many children.

Hallelujah!

Glory be . . . .

(Repeat antiphon)

READING   [1 John 4:16b, 21–5:4]

God is love, and those who abide in love abide in
God, and God abides in them. The commandment
we have from God is this: those who love God must
love their brothers and sisters also.

Everyone who believes that Jesus is the Christ
has been born of God, and everyone who loves the
parent loves the child. By this we know that we love
the children of God, when we love God and obey
God's commandments. And the commandments are
not burdensome, for whatever is born of God conquers the world. And this is the victory that conquers the world, our faith.

(silent reflection)

MAGNIFICAT ANTIPHON

(Ordinary):   When I sought, God answered me,
from all my fears God set me free.

(Advent/Christmas):   The virgin shall bear a son,
who will save the people from their sins.

(Lent):   **The voice of God's word frees us from the darkness.**

(Easter):   **May all those you gave me see this glory of mine, your gift to me.**

MAGNIFICAT

I acclaim the greatness of the Lord,
I delight in God my Savior,
who regarded my humble state.
Truly from this day on
all ages will call me blest.

For God, wonderful in power,
has used that strength for me.
Holy the name of the Lord!
whose mercy embraces the faithful,
one generation to the next.

The mighty arm of God
scatters the proud in their conceit,
pulls tyrants from their thrones,
and raises up the humble.
The Lord fills the starving
and lets the rich go hungry.

God rescues lowly Israel,
recalling the promise of mercy,
the promise made to our ancestors,
to Abraham's heirs for ever.

Glory be . . . .

(Repeat Magnificat antiphon)

INTERCESSIONS

Our Father . . . .

Love eternal, all those around us are gifts of your love. Help us to show obedience to you by loving one another with the pure love of brothers and sisters, especially those whom we find it most difficult to appreciate. Bless our world with peace and justice, Creator, Word and Spirit, who live and reign over all forever. Amen.

May God bless us, deliver us from all evil, and bring us to everlasting life. Amen.

Let us bless God/ and give thanks.

WEEK II—MONDAY
MORNING PRAISE

O God, open my lips,/ and my mouth shall declare your praise. Glory be . . . .

Antiphon

(Ordinary): **Let your love come and I shall live, for your law is my delight.**

(Advent/Christmas): **No one who waits for you shall ever be put to shame.**

(Lent): **Seek the face of God with longing.**

(Easter): **I give you a new commandment: love one another as I have loved you.**

PSALM 36 (35)

**Sin whispers with the wicked,
shares its evil, heart to heart.
These sinners shut their eyes
to all fear of God.
They refuse to see their sin,
to know it and hate it.**

**Their words ring false and empty,
their plans neglect what is good.
They daydream of evil,
plot their crooked ways,
seizing on all that is vile.**

**Your mercy, Lord, spans the sky;
your faithfulness soars among the clouds.**

Your integrity towers like a mountain;
your justice runs deeper than the sea.
Lord, you embrace all life:
How we prize your tender mercy!

God, your people seek shelter,
safe in the warmth of your wings.
They feast at your full table,
slake their thirst in your cool stream,
for you are the fount of life,
you give us light and we see.

Grant mercy always to your own,
victory to honest hearts.
Keep the proud from trampling me,
assaulting me with wicked hands.
Let those sinners collapse,
struck down, never to rise.

(silent reflection)

PSALM 29 (28)

Give the Lord glory, you spirits!
Give glory! Honor God's strength!
Honor the name of the Lord!
Bow when the Lord comes,
majestic and holy.

God's voice thunders
above the massive seas;
powerful, splendid,
God shatters the cedars,
shatters the cedars of Lebanon,
makes Lebanon jump like a calf,
Sirion like a wild ox.

God's voice strikes fire,
makes the desert shudder,
Qadesh shudder in labor,
deer writhe in labor.
God strips the trees.

All shout "Glory!" in your temple, Lord.
For you rule the mighty waters,
you rule over all for ever,
Give strength to your people, Lord,
and bless your people with peace.

Glory be . . . .

(Repeat antiphon)

READING   [Sir 6:18-20, 26-28]

My child, from your youth choose discipline,
    and when you have gray hair you will still find
        wisdom.
Come to her like one who plows and sows,
    and wait for her good harvest.
For when you cultivate her you will toil but little,
    and soon you will eat of her produce.
She seems very harsh to the undisciplined;
    fools cannot remain with her.

Come to her with all your soul,
    and keep her ways with all your might.
Search out and seek, and she will become known to you;
    and when you get hold of her, do not let her go.
For at last you will find the rest she gives,
    and she will be changed into joy for you.

(silent reflection)

BENEDICTUS ANTIPHON

(Ordinary): **God favors those who fear, those who put trust in God's kindness.**

(Advent/Christmas): **God will shower gifts, and our land will yield fruit.**

(Lent): **If today you hear God's voice, harden not your hearts.**

(Easter): **The way we came to understand love was that he laid down his life for us.**

BENEDICTUS

Praise the Lord, the God of Israel,
who shepherds the people and sets them free.

God raises from David's house
a child with power to save.
Through the holy prophets
God promised in ages past
to save us from enemy hands,
from the grip of all who hate us.

The Lord favored our ancestors
recalling the sacred covenant,
the pledge to our ancestor Abraham,
to free us from our enemies,
so we might worship without fear
and be holy and just all our days.

And you, child, will be called
Prophet of the Most High,
for you will come to prepare
a pathway for the Lord

by teaching the people salvation
through forgiveness of their sin.

Out of God's deepest mercy
a dawn will come from on high,
light for those shadowed by death,
a guide for our feet on the way to peace.

Glory be . . . .

(Repeat Benedictus antiphon)

INTERCESSIONS

Our Father . . . .

Holy Wisdom, your ways may be narrow at the outset, but they lead to perfect joy. Strengthen our seeking, increase our desire to lead a more disciplined life, that we may grow closer to you, through Jesus Christ our Lord. Amen.

May God bless us and keep us. May God smile upon us and be gracious to us. May God look upon us kindly, and give us peace. Amen.

Let us bless God/ and give thanks.

WEEK II—MONDAY
EVENING PRAISE

O God, come to my assistance,/ make haste to help me. Glory be . . . .

ANTIPHON

(Ordinary):   My eyes yearn for your saving help, and the promise of your justice.

(Advent/Christmas):   Proclaim to the world that God is ruler; tell all the nations the news of God's love.

(Lent):   Blessed is the servant whom the master finds watching.

(Easter):   All of you who have been baptized into Christ have clothed yourselves with him.

PSALM 115 (114)

Not to us, Lord, not to us,
but to your name give glory,
because of your love,
because of your truth.

Why do the nations say,
"Where is their God?"
Our God is in the heavens
and answers to no one.

Their gods are crafted by hand,
mere silver and gold,
with mouths that are mute
and eyes that are blind,

with ears that are deaf
and noses that cannot smell.

Their hands cannot feel,
their feet cannot walk,
their throats are silent.
Their makers, their worshipers
will be just like them.

Let Israel trust God,
their help and shield.
Let the house of Aaron trust God,
their help and shield.
Let all believers trust God,
their help and shield.

The Lord has remembered us
and will bless us,
will bless the house of Israel,
will bless the house of Aaron.
God will bless all believers,
the small and the great.

May God bless you more and more,
bless all your children.
May you truly be blest
by the maker of heaven and earth.

To the Lord belong the heavens,
to us the earth below!
The dead sing no Hallelujah,
nor do those in the silent ground.
But we will bless you, Lord
now and for ever.

Hallelujah!

(silent reflection)

PSALM 117 (116)

Praise! Give glory to God!
Nations, peoples, give glory!
Strong the love embracing us.
Faithful the Lord for ever.

Hallelujah!

Glory be . . . .

(Repeat antiphon)

READING   [Jas 1:18-25]

In fulfillment of God's own purpose God gave us
birth by the word of truth, so that we would become
a kind of first fruits of God's creatures.

You must understand this, my beloved: let everyone be quick to listen, slow to speak, slow to anger;
for your anger does not produce God's righteousness. Therefore rid yourselves of all sordidness and
rank growth of wickedness, and welcome with meek-
ness the implanted word that has the power to save
your souls. But be doers of the word, and not merely
hearers who deceive themselves. For if any are hearers of the word and not doers, they are like those
who look at themselves in a mirror; for they look at
themselves and, on going away, immediately forget
what they were like. But those who look into the
perfect law, the law of liberty, and persevere, being
not hearers who forget but doers who act—they will
be blessed in their doing.

(silent reflection)

MAGNIFICAT ANTIPHON

(Ordinary):   **Teach me, God, to do your will, for you are my God.**

(Advent/Christmas):   **Let the heavens rejoice and the earth be glad before the Prince of Peace.**

(Lent):   **They who serve me, follow me.**

(Easter):   **All are one in Christ Jesus, alleluia.**

MAGNIFICAT

I acclaim the greatness of the Lord,
I delight in God my Savior,
who regarded my humble state.
Truly from this day on
all ages will call me blest.

For God, wonderful in power,
has used that strength for me.
Holy the name of the Lord!
whose mercy embraces the faithful,
one generation to the next.

The mighty arm of God
scatters the proud in their conceit,
pulls tyrants from their thrones,
and raises up the humble.
The Lord fills the starving
and lets the rich go hungry.

God rescues lowly Israel,
recalling the promise of mercy,
the promise made to our ancestors,
to Abraham's heirs for ever.

Glory be . . . .

(Repeat Magnificat antiphon)

<small>INTERCESSIONS</small>

Our Father . . . .

Living Word, although you have given us abundant tools for doing your will, many good works are left undone. Forgive our failings this day and bring the good we do to perfection in you as we continue to both listen and act. We ask this in your holy name, God, Jesus, Spirit. Amen.

May God bless us, deliver us from all evil, and bring us to everlasting life. Amen.

Let us bless God/ and give thanks.

WEEK II—TUESDAY
MORNING PRAISE

O God, open my lips,/ and my mouth shall declare
your praise. Glory be . . . .

ANTIPHON

(Ordinary):   I shall walk in the path of freedom, for
I seek your precepts.

(Advent/Christmas):   The day of our God is near;
God comes to save us.

(Lent):   When I am lifted up from the earth, I will
draw all people to myself.

(Easter):   The bread I give is my flesh for the life of
the world.

PSALM 23 (22)

The Lord is my shepherd,
I need nothing more.
You give me rest in green meadows,
setting me near calm waters,
where you revive my spirit.

You guide me along sure paths,
you are true to your name.
Though I should walk in death's dark valley,
I fear no evil with you by my side,
your shepherd's staff to comfort me.

You spread a table before me
as my foes look on.
You soothe my head with oil;
my cup is more than full.

Goodness and love will tend me
every day of my life.
I will dwell in the house of the Lord
as long as I shall live.

(silent reflection)

PSALM 57 (56)

Care for me, God, take care of me,
I have nowhere else to hide.
Shadow me with your wings
until all danger passes.

I call to the Most High,
to God, my avenger:
send help from heaven to free me,
punish those who hound me.

Extend to me, O God,
your love that never fails,
for I find myself among lions
who crave for human flesh,
their teeth like spears and arrows,
their tongues sharp as swords.

O God, rise high above the heavens!
Spread your glory across the earth!

They rigged a net for me,
a trap to bring me down;

they dug a pit for me,
but they—they fell in!

I have decided, O God,
my decision is firm:
to you I will sing my praise.
Awake, my soul, to song!

Awake, my harp and lyre,
so I can wake up the dawn!
I will lift my voice in praise,
sing of you, Lord, to all nations.
For your love reaches heaven's edge,
your unfailing love, the skies.

O God, rise high above the heavens!
Spread your glory across the earth!

(silent reflection)

Glory be . . . .

(Repeat antiphon)

READING   [Eph 6:11-17]

Put on the whole armor of God, so that you may be
able to stand against the wiles of the devil. For our
struggle is not against enemies of blood and flesh,
but against the rulers, against the authorities, against
the cosmic powers of this present darkness, against
the spiritual forces of evil in the heavenly places.
Therefore, take up the whole armor of God, so that
you may be able to withstand on that evil day, and
having done everything, to stand firm. Stand therefore, and fasten the belt of truth around your waist,
and put on the breastplate of righteousness. As shoes

for your feet put on whatever will make you ready to proclaim the gospel of peace. With all of these, take the shield of faith, with which you will be able to quench all the flaming arrows of the evil one. Take the helmet of salvation, and the sword of the Spirit, which is the word of God.

(silent reflection)

Benedictus Antiphon

(Ordinary):   **In your great love, answer me, O God, with your help that never fails.**

(Advent/Christmas):   **The people who walked in darkness have seen a great light.**

(Lent):   **Save me, O God, in your steadfast love.**

(Easter):   **All nations, clap your hands. Shout with a voice of joy to God.**

BENEDICTUS

Praise the Lord, the God of Israel,
who shepherds the people and sets them free.

God raises from David's house
a child with power to save.
Through the holy prophets
God promised in ages past
to save us from enemy hands,
from the grip of all who hate us.

The Lord favored our ancestors
recalling the sacred covenant,
the pledge to our ancestor Abraham,

to free us from our enemies,
so we might worship without fear
and be holy and just all our days.

And you, child, will be called
Prophet of the Most High,
for you will come to prepare
a pathway for the Lord
by teaching the people salvation
through forgiveness of their sin.

Out of God's deepest mercy
a dawn will come from on high,
light for those shadowed by death,
a guide for our feet on the way to peace.

Glory be . . . .

(Repeat Benedictus antiphon)

INTERCESSIONS

Our Father . . . .

God of light and truth, we struggle daily against
the evil that is within us and in our world. Clothe
us with the strong and noble armor of virtue that
we might be unswerving in our defense of good, in
the name of Jesus our Lord, through the Holy
Spirit. Amen.

May God bless us and keep us. May God smile
upon us and be gracious to us. May God look upon
us kindly, and give us peace. Amen.

Let us bless God/ and give thanks.

WEEK II—TUESDAY
EVENING PRAISE

O God, come to my assistance,/ make haste to help me. Glory be . . . .

ANTIPHON

(Ordinary): I am your servant, give me knowledge; then I shall know your will.

(Advent/Christmas): Come, O Savior, do not delay; forgive the sins of your people.

(Lent): We preach a Christ who was crucified; he is the power and the wisdom of God.

(Easter): I am with you always, until the end of the world.

PSALM 132 (131)

Lord, remember David
in all his humility.
He swore an oath to you,
O Mighty God of Jacob:

"I will not enter my home,
nor lie down on my bed.
I will not close my eyes
nor will I sleep
until I find a place for the Lord,
a house for the Mighty God of Jacob."

We heard about it in Ephrata,
in the fields of Yaarim:
"Let us go to God's house,
let us worship at God's throne."

Lord, come to your resting place,
you and your ark of power.
May your priests dress for the feast,
and your faithful shout for joy.

Be loyal to David, your servant,
do not reject your anointed.
You once swore to David
and will not break your word:
"Your child will ascend your throne.

"If your heirs then keep my laws,
if they keep my covenant,
their children will rule
from your throne for ever."

The Lord has chosen Zion,
desired it as a home.
"This is my resting place,
I choose to live here for ever.

"I will bless it with abundance,
even the poor will have food.
I will vest the priests in holiness,
and the faithful will shout for joy.

"Here I will strengthen David's power
and light a lamp for my anointed.
His enemies I will clothe in shame,
but on him a crown will shine."

(silent reflection)

PSALM 126 (125)

The Lord brings us back to Zion,
we are like dreamers,
laughing, dancing,
with songs on our lips.

Other nations say,
"A new world of wonders!
The Lord is with them."
Yes, God works wonders.
Rejoice! Be glad!

Lord, bring us back
as water to thirsty land.
Those sowing in tears
reap, singing and laughing.

They left weeping, weeping,
casting the seed.
They come back singing, singing,
holding high the harvest.

Glory be . . . .

(Repeat antiphon)

READING   [Mic 6:6-8]

"With what shall I come before the LORD,
    and bow myself before God on high?
Shall I come before him with burnt offerings,
    with calves a year old?
Will the LORD be pleased with thousands of rams,
    with ten thousands of rivers of oil?
Shall I give my firstborn for my transgression,
    the fruit of my body for the sin of my soul?"

He has told you, O mortal, what is good;
  and what does the LORD require of you
but to do justice, and to love kindness,
  and to walk humbly with your God?

(silent reflection)

MAGNIFICAT ANTIPHON

(Ordinary):   I obey your precepts and your will; all
that I do is before you.

(Advent/Christmas):   Behold, our God shall come
with power, will enlighten the eyes of your servants.

(Lent):   The salvation of the just comes from God,
their strength in time of need.

(Easter):   God is my light and my salvation; of
whom should I be afraid?

MAGNIFICAT

I acclaim the greatness of the Lord,
I delight in God my Savior,
who regarded my humble state.
Truly from this day on
all ages will call me blest.

For God, wonderful in power,
has used that strength for me.
Holy the name of the Lord!
whose mercy embraces the faithful,
one generation to the next.

The mighty arm of God
scatters the proud in their conceit,

pulls tyrants from their thrones,
and raises up the humble.
The Lord fills the starving
and lets the rich go hungry.

God rescues lowly Israel,
recalling the promise of mercy,
the promise made to our ancestors,
to Abraham's heirs for ever.

Glory be . . . .

(Repeat Magnificat antiphon)

INTERCESSIONS

Our Father . . . .

God of justice, You are most present in the weak of
the world. Help us to welcome the poor and the
sick, the young and the old, the stranger and those
who are the least among us, as we would welcome
Christ. May we walk humbly with you in the ways
of love and righteousness, through Christ your Son
in union with the Spirit. Amen.

May God bless us, deliver us from all evil, and
bring us to everlasting life. Amen.

Let us bless God/ and give thanks.

WEEK II—WEDNESDAY
MORNING PRAISE

O God, open my lips,/ and my mouth shall declare your praise. Glory be . . . .

(Ordinary):   **God is kind and full of compassion, slow to anger, abounding in love.**

(Advent/Christmas):   **We await the coming of God who is justice.**

(Lent):   **Rid yourselves of all your sins; make a new heart and a new spirit.**

(Easter):   **Who is the King of Glory? It is Christ the Lord.**

PSALM 65 (64)

**Praise is yours, God in Zion.
Now is the moment
to keep our vow,
for you, God, are listening.**

**All people come to you
bringing their shameful deeds.
You free us from guilt,
from overwhelming sin.**

**Happy are those you invite
and then welcome to your courts.**

Fill us with the plenty of your house,
the holiness of your temple.

You give victory
in answer to our prayer.
You inspire awe, God, our savior,
hope of distant lands and waters.

Clothed in power,
you steady the mountains;
you still the roaring seas,
restless waves, raging nations.
People everywhere
stand amazed at what you do,
east and west shout for joy.

You tend and water the land.
How wonderful the harvest!
You fill your springs,
ready the seeds, prepare the grain.

You soak the furrows
and level the ridges.
With softening rain
you bless the land with growth.

You crown the year with riches.
All you touch comes alive:
untilled lands yield crops,
hills are dressed in joy,

flocks clothe the pastures,
valleys wrap themselves in grain.
They all shout for joy
and break into song.

(silent reflection)

PSALM 84 (83)

Your temple is my joy,
Lord of heaven's might.
I am eager for it,
eager for the courts of God.
My flesh, my flesh sings
its joy to the living God.

As a sparrow homing,
a swallow seeking a nest
to hatch its young,
I am eager for your altars,
Lord of heaven's might,
My king, my God.

To live with you is joy,
to praise you and never stop.
Those you bless with courage
will bless you from their hearts.

When they cross the Valley of Thirst
the ground is spaced with springs,
with the welcome rain of autumn.
They travel the towns to reach
the God of gods in Zion.

Hear me, Lord of might;
hear me, God of Jacob.
God our shield, look,
see the face of your anointed.

One day within your courts
is worth a thousand without.
I would rather stand at God's gate
than move among the wicked.

God is our sun, our shield,
the giver of honor and grace.
The Lord never fails to bless
those who walk with integrity.
Lord of heaven's might,
blest are all who trust in you.

Glory be . . . .

(Repeat antiphon)

READING   [Isa 42:5-9]

Thus says God, the LORD,
    who created the heavens and stretched them out,
    who spread out the earth and what comes from it,
who gives breath to the people upon it
    and spirit to those who walk in it:
I am the LORD, I have called you in righteousness,
    I have taken you by the hand and kept you;
I have given you as a covenant to the people,
    a light to the nations,
    to open the eyes that are blind,
to bring out the prisoners from the dungeon,
    from the prison those who sit in darkness.
I am the LORD, that is my name;
    my glory I give to no other,
    nor my praise to idols.
See, the former things have come to pass,
    and new things I now declare;
before they spring forth,
    I tell you of them.

(silent reflection)

BENEDICTUS ANTIPHON

(Ordinary):   **A pure heart create for me, O God; put a steadfast spirit within me.**

(Advent/Christmas):   **All flesh shall see the salvation of God.**

(Lent):   **Your words, O God, are spirit and life; you have the words of eternal life.**

(Easter):   **All you nations, sing out your joy to God, alleluia, alleluia.**

BENEDICTUS

**Praise the Lord, the God of Israel,
who shepherds the people and sets them free.**

**God raises from David's house
a child with power to save.
Through the holy prophets
God promised in ages past
to save us from enemy hands,
from the grip of all who hate us.**

**The Lord favored our ancestors
recalling the sacred covenant,
the pledge to our ancestor Abraham,
to free us from our enemies,
so we might worship without fear
and be holy and just all our days.**

**And you, child, will be called
Prophet of the Most High,
for you will come to prepare
a pathway for the Lord**

by teaching the people salvation
through forgiveness of their sin.

Out of God's deepest mercy
a dawn will come from on high,
light for those shadowed by death,
a guide for our feet on the way to peace.

Glory be . . . .

(Repeat Benedictus antiphon)

INTERCESSIONS

Our Father . . . .

Eternal light, you want all creation to live in harmony.
Grace us with the instruments of good works and
the desire to use them to build your kingdom
among us. We pray this through Christ and in the
Spirit. Amen.

May God bless us and keep us. May God smile
upon us and be gracious to us. May God look upon
us kindly, and give us peace. Amen.

Let us bless God/ and give thanks.

WEEK II—WEDNESDAY
EVENING PRAYER

O God, come to my assistance,/ make haste to help me. Glory be . . . .

ANTIPHON

(Ordinary):   **Give thanks, for God is good, is lasting love.**

(Advent/Christmas):   **God will come to save all nations, and your hearts will exult to hear the majestic voice.**

(Lent):   **My soul is thirsting for the living God.**

(Easter):   **This is how all will know you for my disciples: your love for one another.**

PSALM 12 (11)

Help us, Lord,
for no one stays loyal,
the faithful have vanished.
People lie to each other,
no one speaks from the heart.

May the Lord silence
the smooth tongue
and boasting lips that say:
"Our words will triumph!
With weapons like these
who can master us?"

Then the Lord speaks out:
"I will act now,
for the poor are broken
and the needy groan.
When they call out,
I will protect them."

The Lord's word is pure,
like silver from the furnace,
seven times refined.

Lord, keep your promise,
always protect your own.
Guard them from this age
when wickedness abounds
and evil is prized above all.

(silent reflection)

PSALM 135 (134)

Hallelujah!

Praise the name of the Lord,
give praise, faithful servants,
who stand in the courtyard,
gathered at God's house.

Sing hymns for God is good.
Sing God's name, our delight,
for the Lord chose Jacob,
Israel as a special treasure.

I know the Lord is great,
surpassing every little god.
What God wills, God does

in heaven and earth,
in the deepest sea.

God blankets earth with clouds,
strikes lightning for the rain,
releases wind from the storehouse.

God killed Egypt's firstborn,
both humans and beasts,
doing wondrous signs in Egypt
against Pharaoh and his aides.

God struck down nations,
killed mighty kings,
Sihon, king of the Amorites,
Og, king of Bashan,
all the kings of Canaan.

Then God gave Israel their land,
a gift for them to keep.
Your name lives for ever, Lord,
your renown never fades,
for you give your people justice
and attend to their needs.

Pagan idols are silver and gold
crafted by human hands.
Their mouths cannot speak,
their eyes do not see.

Their ears hear nothing,
their nostrils do not breathe.
Their makers who rely on them
become like these hollow images.

Bless God, house of Israel,
house of Aaron, house of Levi,
every faithful one.

**Blest be the Lord of Zion,
who calls Jerusalem home.**

Hallelujah!

Glory be . . . .

(Repeat antiphon)

READING   [Phil 4:4-9]

Rejoice in the Lord always; again I will say, rejoice.
Let your gentleness be known to everyone. The Lord
is near. Do not worry about anything, but in everything by prayer and supplication with thanksgiving
let your requests be made known to God. And the
peace of God, which surpasses all understanding, will
guard your hearts and your minds in Christ Jesus.

Finally, beloved, whatever is true, whatever is hon-
orable, whatever is just, whatever is pure, whatever is
pleasing, whatever is commendable, if there is any
excellence and if there is anything worthy of praise,
think about these things. Keep on doing the things
that you have learned and received and heard and
seen in me, and the God of peace will be with you.

(silent reflection)

MAGNIFICAT ANTIPHON

(Ordinary):   **God is good to those who hope, to
those who are searching for God's love.**

(Advent/Christmas):   **Today you will know that our
God is coming to save us, and in the morning you
will see the glory.**

(Lent):   I live by faith in the Son of God, who loved me and sacrificed himself for me.

(Easter):   God shall dwell with us, and we shall be God's people.

MAGNIFICAT

I acclaim the greatness of the Lord,
I delight in God my Savior,
who regarded my humble state.
Truly from this day on
all ages will call me blest.

For God, wonderful in power,
has used that strength for me.
Holy the name of the Lord!
whose mercy embraces the faithful,
one generation to the next.

The mighty arm of God
scatters the proud in their conceit,
pulls tyrants from their thrones,
and raises up the humble.
The Lord fills the starving
and lets the rich go hungry.

God rescues lowly Israel,
recalling the promise of mercy,
the promise made to our ancestors,
to Abraham's heirs for ever.

Glory be . . . .

(Repeat Magnificat antiphon)

INTERCESSIONS

Our Father . . . .

God our greatest joy, we rejoice that you call all peoples to live in peace and in happiness. Teach us to trust you and each other that we might be free from worry and fear. May we ever seek peace and pursue it, in your holy name, Creator, Redeemer and Spirit. Amen.

May God bless us, deliver us from all evil, and bring us to everlasting life. Amen.

Let us bless God/ and give thanks.

WEEK II—THURSDAY
MORNING PRAISE

O God, open my lips,/ and my mouth shall declare you praise. Glory be . . . .

ANTIPHON

(Ordinary):   Anyone who loves God will be true to God's word.

(Advent/Christmas):   Rise up, Jerusalem, stand on the heights and see the joy that is coming to you from God.

(Lent):   Unless a grain of wheat falls to the earth and dies, it remains a single grain.

(Easter):   You are the source of life, and in the light of your glory we find happiness.

PSALM 88 (87)

Save me, Lord my God!
By day, by night, I cry out.
Let my prayer reach you;
turn, listen to me.

I am steeped in trouble,
ready for the grave.
I am like one destined for the pit,
a warrior deprived of strength,
forgotten among the dead,
buried with the slaughtered
for whom you care no more.

You tossed me to the bottom of the pit,
into its murky darkness,
your anger pulled me down
like roaring waves.

You took my friends away,
disgraced me before them.
Trapped here with no escape,
I cannot see beyond my pain.

Lord, I cry out to you all day,
my hands keep reaching out.
Do you work marvels for the dead?
Can shadows rise and sing praise?

Is your mercy sung in the grave,
your lasting love in Sheol?
Are your wonders known in the pit?
your justice, in forgotten places?

But I cry out to you, God,
each morning I plead with you.
Why do you reject me, Lord?
Why do you hide your face?

Weak since childhood,
I am often close to death.
Your torments track me down,
your rage consumes me,
your trials destroy me.

All day, they flood around me,
pressing down, closing me in.
You took my friends from me;
darkness is all I have left.

(silent reflection)

PSALM 123 (122)

I gaze at the heavens,
searching for you, my God.

A slave watches his master's hand,
a servant girl, the hand of her mistress;
so our eyes rest on you, Lord,
awaiting your kindness.

Have mercy, God, have mercy.
We have swallowed enough scorn,
stomached enough sneers:
the scoffing of the complacent,
the mockery of the proud.

Glory be . . . .

(Repeat antiphon)

READING   [Wis 1:11-15]

Beware then of useless grumbling
and keep your tongue from slander;
because no secret word is without result,
and a lying mouth destroys the soul.
Do not invite death by the error of your life,
or bring on destruction by the works of your hands;
because God did not make death and does not delight
    in the death of the living.
For God created all things so that they might exist;
the generative forces of the world are wholesome,
and there is no destructive poison in them,
and the dominion of Hades is not on earth.
For righteousness is immortal.

(silent reflection)

BENEDICTUS ANTIPHON

(Ordinary):   **Drink in the richness of God, enjoy the strength of the Lord.**

(Advent/Christmas):   **Be strong and fear not, our God will come to save us.**

(Lent):   **I shall not die but live to tell the Lord's great deeds.**

(Easter):   **I came that you may have life, and have it to the full.**

BENEDICTUS

Praise the Lord, the God of Israel,
who shepherds the people and sets them free.

God raises from David's house
a child with power to save.
Through the holy prophets
God promised in ages past
to save us from enemy hands,
from the grip of all who hate us.

The Lord favored our ancestors
recalling the sacred covenant,
the pledge to our ancestor Abraham,
to free us from our enemies,
so we might worship without fear
and be holy and just all our days.

And you, child, will be called
Prophet of the Most High,
for you will come to prepare
a pathway for the Lord

by teaching the people salvation
through forgiveness of their sin.

Out of God's deepest mercy
a dawn will come from on high,
light for those shadowed by death,
a guide for our feet on the way to peace.

Glory be . . . .

(Repeat Benedictus antiphon)

INTERCESSIONS

Our Father . . . .

Fount of life, bless our works and our words this
day that, free of destructive acts and attitudes, we
might show the inner peace of our hearts through
fruitful labor and gentle speech. Teach us your way
of righteousness, Creator, Redeemer and Spirit.
Amen.

May God bless us and keep us. May God smile
upon us and be gracious to us. May God look upon
us kindly, and give us peace. Amen.

Let us bless God/ and give thanks.

WEEK II—THURSDAY
EVENING PRAISE

O God, come to my assistance,/ make haste to help me. Glory be . . . .

ANTIPHON

(Ordinary): **Keep alert, for you do not know when the time will come.**

(Advent/Christmas): **This is the name they give him: Wonder-Counsellor, Mighty-God, Eternal-Father, Prince-of-Peace.**

(Lent): **Be glad to share in the sufferings of Christ! When he comes in glory, you will be filled with joy.**

(Easter): **May all the earth give you worship and praise.**

PSALM 140 (139)

Rescue me, Lord, from the wicked,
save me from the violent.
They spawn evil in their hearts,
starting fights every day.
Their tongues strike like a serpent,
their lips hide deadly venom.

Free me, Lord, from their evil,
save me from the violent
who plot my downfall.
The arrogant hide their traps,

and set their snares for me,
tangling my path with nets.

But you, Lord, are my God.
Listen! I plead with you.
Be the fort that saves me, Lord,
my helmet when the battle comes.

Do not side with the wicked,
do not let their plots succeed
or they will prevail.
They connive to entrap me,
let them drown in their venom!

Heap hot coals upon them,
plunge them into the deep,
never to rise again.
Let liars find no place to rest,
let evil stalk the violent
and drive them to their ruin.

I know how the Lord acts,
judging for the weak,
vindicating the poor.
The just honor your name,
the innocent live in your sight.

(silent reflection)

PSALM 62 (61)

My soul waits, silent for God,
for God alone, my salvation,
alone my rock, my safety,
my refuge: I stand secure.

How long will some of you attack
tearing others down
as if walls or fences
on the verge of collapse?

You scheme to topple them,
so smug in your lies;
your lips are all blessing,
but murder fills your heart.

Wait, my soul, silent for God,
for God alone, my hope,
alone my rock, my safety,
my refuge: I stand secure.

God is my glory and safety,
my stronghold, my haven.
People, give your hearts to God,
trust always! God is our haven.

Mortals are but a breath,
nothing more than a mirage;
set them on the scales,
they prove lighter than mist.

Avoid extortion and fraud,
the hopes they breed are nothing;
and if you should grow rich,
place no trust in wealth.

Time and again God said,
"Strength and love are mine to give."
The Lord repays us all
in light of what we do.

Glory be . . . .

(Repeat antiphon)

READING [Acts 2:41a, 42-47]

So those who welcomed his message were baptized.
They devoted themselves to the apostles' teaching and
fellowship, to the breaking of bread and the prayers.

Awe came upon everyone, because many wonders
and signs were being done by the apostles. All who
believed were together and had all things in common:
they would sell their possessions and goods and dis-
tribute the proceeds to all, as any had need. Day by
day, they spent much time together in the temple, they
broke bread at home and ate their food with glad and
generous hearts, praising God and having the good-
will of all the people. And day by day the Lord added
to their number those who were being saved.

(silent reflection)

MAGNIFICAT ANTIPHON

(Ordinary): **May the God of peace make you perfect
and holy.**

(Advent/Christmas): **With justice God will rule the
world, will judge the peoples with truth.**

(Lent): **Blessed are the poor in spirit; the kingdom
of heaven is theirs.**

(Easter): **God has prepared a feast for me.**

MAGNIFICAT

I acclaim the greatness of the Lord,
I delight in God my Savior,
who regarded my humble state.
Truly from this day on
all ages will call me blest.

For God, wonderful in power,
has used that strength for me.
Holy the name of the Lord!
whose mercy embraces the faithful,
one generation to the next.

The mighty arm of God
scatters the proud in their conceit,
pulls tyrants from their thrones,
and raises up the humble.
The Lord fills the starving
and lets the rich go hungry.

God rescues lowly Israel,
recalling the promise of mercy,
the promise made to our ancestors,
to Abraham's heirs for ever.

Glory be . . . .

(Repeat Magnificat antiphon)

INTERCESSIONS

Our Father . . . .

Generous God, help us to live in unity and generosity. May our possessions not dominate our lives. May we rejoice when needing little and be humbled by our weakness when wanting more. Gather all people together into you, our triune God, forever and ever. Amen.

May God bless us, deliver us from all evil, and bring us to everlasting life. Amen.

Let us bless God/ and give thanks.

WEEK II—FRIDAY
MORNING PRAISE

O God, open my lips,/ and my mouth shall declare your praise. Glory be . . . .

ANTIPHON

(Ordinary):   **Those you bless with courage will bless you from their hearts.**

(Advent/Christmas):   **No ear has heard, no eye has seen any other good act like this for those who trust.**

(Lent):   **There is no greater love than this: to lay down one's life for one's friends.**

(Easter):   **God loved the world so much as to give the only Son.**

PSALM 16 (15)

Protect me, God,
I turn to you for help.
I profess, "You are my Lord,
my greatest good."

I once put faith in false gods,
the idols of the land.
Now I make no offering to them,
nor invoke their names.
Those who chase after them
add grief upon grief.

Lord, you measure out my portion,
the shape of my future;

you mark off the best place for me
to enjoy my inheritance.

I bless God who teaches me,
who schools my heart even at night.
I am sure God is here,
right beside me.
I cannot be shaken.

So my heart rejoices,
my body thrills with life,
my whole being rests secure.

You will not abandon me to Sheol,
nor send your faithful one to death.
You show me the road to life:
boundless joy at your side for ever!

(silent reflection)

PSALM 92 (91)

How good to thank you, Lord,
to praise your name, Most High,
to sing your love at dawn,
your faithfulness at dusk
with sound of lyre and harp,
with music of the lute.
For your work brings delight,
your deeds invite song.

I marvel at what you do.
Lord, how deep your thought!
Fools do not grasp this
nor the senseless understand.
Scoundrels spring up like grass,

flourish and quickly wither.
You, Lord, stand firm for ever.

See how your enemies perish,
scattered to the winds,
while you give me brute strength
pouring rich oil upon me.
I have faced my enemies,
heard them plot against me.

The just grow tall like palm trees,
majestic like cedars of Lebanon.
They are planted in the temple courts
and flourish in God's house,
green and heavy with fruit
even in old age.

Proclaim that God is just,
my rock without a fault.

Glory be . . . .

(Repeat antiphon)

READING   [Hos 14:1, 4-9]

Return, O Israel, to the Lord your God,
    for you have stumbled because of your iniquity.
I will heal their disloyalty;
    I will love them freely,
    for my anger has turned from them.
I will be like the dew to Israel;
    he shall blossom like the lily,
    he shall strike root like the forests of Lebanon.
His shoots shall spread out;
    his beauty shall be like the olive tree,
    and his fragrance like that of Lebanon.

They shall again live beneath my shadow,
    they shall flourish as a garden;
    they shall blossom like the wine of Lebanon.
Those who are wise understand these things;
    those who are discerning know them.
For the ways of the Lord are right,
    and the upright walk in them,
    but transgressors stumble in them.

(silent reflection)

BENEDICTUS ANTIPHON

(Ordinary):   God of heaven's might, blest are all
who trust in you.

(Advent/Christmas):   God of hosts, bring us back; let
your face shine on us and we shall be saved.

(Lent):   Those who have left everything and followed
me will gain eternal life.

(Easter):   I believe you are the Christ, the Son of God.

BENEDICTUS

Praise the Lord, the God of Israel,
who shepherds the people and sets them free.

God raises from David's house
a child with power to save.
Through the holy prophets
God promised in ages past
to save us from enemy hands,
from the grip of all who hate us.

The Lord favored our ancestors
recalling the sacred covenant,

the pledge to our ancestor Abraham,
to free us from our enemies,
so we might worship without fear
and be holy and just all our days.

And you, child, will be called
Prophet of the Most High,
for you will come to prepare
a pathway for the Lord
by teaching the people salvation
through forgiveness of their sin.

Out of God's deepest mercy
a dawn will come from on high,
light for those shadowed by death,
a guide for our feet on the way to peace.

Glory be . . . .

(Repeat Benedictus antiphon)

INTERCESSIONS

Our Father . . . .

Forgiving God, the death of your son brought new
life to a sinful people. Support us in our wavering,
console us in our sorrow, and help us to daily begin
anew through the death and resurrection of Jesus,
who lives and reigns with you and the Holy Spirit.
Amen.

May God bless us and keep us. May God smile
upon us and be gracious to us. May God look upon
us kindly, and give us peace. Amen.

Let us bless God/ and give thanks.

WEEK II—FRIDAY
EVENING PRAISE

O God, come to my assistance,/ make haste to help me. Glory be . . . .

ANTIPHON

(Ordinary): **Let my prayer come before you; incline your ear to my cry.**

(Advent/Christmas): **Say to the cities of Judah, "Here is your God."**

(Lent): **He has truly borne our sufferings, has carried all our sorrows.**

(Easter): **The Son of Man came to give his life as ransom for the many.**

PSALM 22 (21)

God, my God,
why have you abandoned me—
far from my cry, my words of pain?
I call by day, you do not answer.
I call by night, but find no rest.

You are the Holy One enthroned,
the Praise of Israel.
Our people trusted, they trusted you;
you rescued them.
To you they cried, and they were saved;
they trusted and were not shamed.

But I am a worm, hardly human,
despised by all, mocked by the crowd.
All who see me jeer at me,
sneer at me, shaking their heads:
"You relied on God; let God help you!
If God loves you, let God save you!"

But you, God, took me from the womb,
you kept me safe at my mother's breast.
I belonged to you from the time of birth,
you are my God from my mother's womb.

Do not stay far off,
danger is so close.
I have no other help.
Wild bulls surround me,
bulls of Bashan encircle me,
opening their jaws against me
like roaring, ravening lions.

I am poured out like water,
my bones are pulled apart,
my heart is wax melting within me,
my throat baked and dry,
my tongue stuck to my jaws.
You bring me down to the dust of death.

There are dogs all around me,
a pack of villains corners me.
They tear my hands and feet,
I can count all my bones.
They stare at me and gloat.
They take what I wore,
they roll dice for my clothes.

Lord, do not stay far off,
you, my strength, be quick to help.
Save my neck from the sword,
save my life from the dog's teeth,
save me from the lion's jaws,
save me from the bull's horns.
You hear me.

(silent reflection)

PSALM 22 (21) continued

I will proclaim your name to my people,
I will praise you in the assembly.

Give praise, all who fear God:
revere and honor the Lord,
children of Israel, people of Jacob.
The Lord never scorns the afflicted,
never looks away, but hears their cry.

I will sing of you in the great assembly,
make good my promise before your faithful.
The poor shall eat all they want.
Seekers of God shall give praise.
"May your hearts live for ever!"

All peoples shall remember and turn,
all races will bow to the Lord,
who holds dominion over nations.
The well-fed crowd kneel before God,
all destined to die bow low.

My soul lives for the Lord!
My children will serve,

will proclaim God to the future,
announcing to peoples yet unborn,
"God saves."

Glory be . . . .

(Repeat antiphon)

READING   [Heb 5:1-4, 7-9]

Every high priest chosen from among mortals is
put in charge of things pertaining to God on their be-
half, to offer gifts and sacrifices for sins. He is able to
deal gently with the ignorant and wayward, since he
himself is subject to weakness; and because of this he
must offer sacrifice for his own sins as well as for
those of the people. And one does not presume to
take this honor, but takes it only when called by God,
just as Aaron was.

In the days of his flesh, Jesus offered up prayers
and supplications, with loud cries and tears, to the
one who was able to save him from death, and he was
heard because of his reverent submission. Although
he was a Son, he learned obedience through what he
suffered; and having been made perfect, he became
the source of eternal salvation for all who obey him.

(silent reflection)

MAGNIFICAT ANTIPHON

(Ordinary):   **God delights in saving a helpless people.**

(Advent/Christmas):   **Faithfulness shall spring from
the earth and justice look down from heaven.**

(Lent): **What return can I make for all that God has done for me?**

(Easter): **Christ loved us and gave himself up for us as a fragrant offering to God.**

MAGNIFICAT

**I acclaim the greatness of the Lord,
I delight in God my Savior,
who regarded my humble state.
Truly from this day on
all ages will call me blest.**

**For God, wonderful in power,
has used that strength for me.
Holy the name of the Lord!
whose mercy embraces the faithful,
one generation to the next.**

**The mighty arm of God
scatters the proud in their conceit,
pulls tyrants from their thrones,
and raises up the humble.
The Lord fills the starving
and lets the rich go hungry.**

**God rescues lowly Israel,
recalling the promise of mercy,
the promise made to our ancestors,
to Abraham's heirs for ever.**

Glory be . . . .

(Repeat Magnificat antiphon)

INTERCESSIONS

Our Father . . . .

Mighty God, your son was obedient to your will even to death. Grant us wisdom and humility when we hold authority over others and when we must be submissive to others. May we listen obediently whenever and through whomever you come to us, triune God, forever. Amen.

May God bless us, deliver us from all evil, and bring us to everlasting life. Amen.

Let us bless God/ and give thanks.

WEEK II—SATURDAY
MORNING PRAISE

O God, open my lips,/ and my mouth shall declare your praise. Glory be . . . .

ANTIPHON

(Ordinary):   **God, keep watch over my thought and word.**

(Advent/Christmas):   **Come, Wisdom of our God Most High, teach us to walk in paths of knowledge.**

(Lent):   **Look for the power, look for the presence of God.**

(Easter):   **Alleluia! Truth and beauty surround him.**

PSALM 96 (95)

**A new song for the Lord!
Sing it and bless God's name,
everyone, everywhere!
Tell the whole world
God's triumph day to day,
God's glory, God's wonder.**

**A noble God deserving praise,
the dread of other gods,
the puny gods of pagans;
for our God made the heavens—
the Lord of majestic light
who fills the temple with beauty.**

Proclaim the Lord, you nations,
praise the glory of God's power,
praise the glory of God's name!
Bring gifts to the temple,
bow down, all the earth,
tremble in God's holy presence.

Tell the nations, "The Lord rules!"
As the firm earth is not swayed,
nothing can sway God's judgment.
Let heaven and earth be glad,
the sea and sea creatures roar,
the field and its beasts exult.

Then let the trees of the forest sing
before the coming of the Lord,
who comes to judge the nations,
to set the earth aright,
restoring the world to order.

(silent reflection)

PSALM 108 (107)

I have decided, O God,
I will sing of your glory,
will sing your praise.
Awake, my harp and lyre,
so I can wake up the dawn.

I will lift my voice,
sing of you, Lord, to all nations.
For your love fills the heavens,
your unfailing love, the sky.

O God, rise high above the heavens!
Spread your glory across the earth!
Deliver those you love,
use your strength to rescue me.

God decreed in the temple:
"I give away Shechem,
parcel out Succoth.
Manasseh and Gilead are mine.

"With Ephraim as my helmet,
and Judah my spear,
I will make Moab my wash bowl,
trample Edom under my feet,
and over Philistia shout in triumph."

Who will help me, Lord,
scale the heights of Edom
and breach the city wall?
God, will you keep holding back?
Will you desert our camp?

Stand by us against the enemy,
all other aid is worthless.
With you the battle is ours,
you will crush our foes.

Glory be . . . .

(Repeat antiphon)

READING   [Zech 14:8-9, 11, 20-21a]

On that day living waters shall flow out from
Jerusalem, half of them to the eastern sea and half of

them to the western sea; it shall continue in summer
as in winter.

And the LORD will become king over all the earth;
on that day the LORD will be one and God's name one.
And [Jerusalem] shall be inhabited, for never again
shall it be doomed to destruction; Jerusalem shall abide
in security.

On that day there shall be inscribed on the bells of
the horses, "Holy to the LORD." And the cooking pots
in the house of the LORD shall be as holy as the bowls
in front of the altar; and every cooking pot in Jerusalem and Judah shall be sacred to the LORD of hosts.

(silent reflection)

BENEDICTUS ANTIPHON

(Ordinary):   I give thanks to your name for your
love and fidelity.

(Advent/Christmas):   Come, Key of David, free the
prisoners of darkness.

(Lent):   They are wise who depend on God, who
look to Israel's maker.

(Easter):   Praise God's name, at whose word you
came forth.

BENEDICTUS

Praise the Lord, the God of Israel,
who shepherds the people and sets them free.

God raises from David's house
a child with power to save.

Through the holy prophets
God promised in ages past
to save us from enemy hands,
from the grip of all who hate us.

The Lord favored our ancestors
recalling the sacred covenant,
the pledge to our ancestor Abraham,
to free us from our enemies,
so we might worship without fear
and be holy and just all our days.

And you, child, will be called
Prophet of the Most High,
for you will come to prepare
a pathway for the Lord
by teaching the people salvation
through forgiveness of their sin.

Out of God's deepest mercy
a dawn will come from on high,
light for those shadowed by death,
a guide for our feet on the way to peace.

Glory be . . . .

(Repeat Benedictus antiphon)

INTERCESSIONS

Our Father . . . .

Creator, your faithful ones await the fulfillment of
your kingdom. Help us to witness that it has begun
and is present among us by the reverence with
which we treat creation. Keep us mindful that

everything is holy to you and that all people and things are vessels of your presence, who live and reign forever. Amen.

May God bless us and keep us. May God smile upon us and be gracious to us. May God look upon us kindly, and give us peace. Amen.

Let us bless God/ and give thanks.

MAJOR FEASTS OF
THE CHURCH YEAR

Below is a list of some of the major feasts of the Church
year. Also included are a limited number of other pop-
ular saints' feast days and feasts which are especially
remembered among those who follow the Benedictine
way of life. On these days a special version of the
Liturgy of the Hours may be prayed to commemorate
the person or feast. One may also wish to commemorate other saints not listed here, such as the patron of
an individual or of a praying community, by using the
common of saints on his or her feast day.

JANUARY
1   Solemnity of Mary
2   Basil and Gregory Nazianzen, writers on the
    ascetical life
15 Maur and Placid, disciples of Benedict
17 Antony, abbot, early monastic founder
21 Meinrad, hermit and martyr of hospitality
25 Conversion of Paul the Apostle
26 Robert, Alberic, Stephen, first Cistercian abbots

FEBRUARY
2   Presentation of Jesus
10 Scholastica, sister of Benedict
11 Benedict of Aniane, abbot
    Our Lady of Lourdes
22 Chair of Peter, the Apostle
25 Walburga, abbess and missionary

MARCH
9   Frances of Rome, patroness of Benedictine oblates

17   Patrick
19   Joseph
21   Passing of Benedict
25   Annunciation of the Lord

APRIL
21   Anselm, Benedictine bishop and doctor of the
     Church
25   Mark, Evangelist

MAY
 1   Joseph the Worker
 3   Philip and James, apostles
11   Odo, Maiolus, Odilo, Hugh and Peter the
     Venerable, abbots of Cluny
14   Matthias, apostle
15   Pachomius, early monastic founder
25   Bede the Venerable, monk and doctor of the
     Church
27   Augustine of Canterbury
31   Visitation

JUNE
 5   Boniface, martyred monastic missionary
11   Barnabas, apostle
13   Anthony of Padua
19   Romuald, founder of Camaldolese Benedictines
23   Sacred Heart
24   Birth of John the Baptist
29   Peter and Paul, apostles

JULY
 3   Thomas, apostle
11   Benedict
13   Henry, emperor and patron of Benedictine
     oblates

22   Mary Magdalene
25   James, apostle
26   Joachim and Ann
29   Martha, Mary, Lazarus

AUGUST
 6   Transfiguration
 8   Dominic
10   Lawrence, martyr
11   Clare of Assisi
15   Assumption of Mary
20   Bernard, abbot and doctor of the Church
24   Bartholomew, apostle
28   Augustine of Hippo
29   Beheading of John the Baptist

SEPTEMBER
 3   Gregory the Great, pope and biographer of
     Benedict
 8   Birth of Mary
14   Triumph of the Holy Cross
17   Hildegarde, abbess and scholar
21   Matthew, apostle and evangelist
29   Michael and all angels
30   Jerome, monk and doctor of the Church

OCTOBER
 1   Therese of the Child Jesus
 2   Guardian Angels
 4   Francis of Assisi
 7   Our Lady of the Rosary
15   Teresa of Jesus, doctor of the Church
18   Luke, evangelist
28   Simon and Jude, apostles

NOVEMBER

1	All Saints
2	All Souls
9	Dedication of St. John Lateran
11	Martin of Tours, bishop
16	Gertrude the Great, nun and spiritual writer
19	Mechtild, nun and companion of Gertrude
21	Presentation of Mary
22	Cecilia, martyr
26	Sylvester, Benedictine abbot
30	Andrew, apostle

DECEMBER

6	Nicholas
8	Immaculate Conception
13	Lucy, martyr
25	Christmas
26	Stephen, martyr
27	John, apostle and evangelist
28	Holy Innocents, martyrs

COMMON FOR FEASTS OF CHRIST
MORNING PRAISE

O God, open my lips,/ and my mouth shall declare your praise. Glory be . . . .

ANTIPHON

Just as in Adam all die, so in Christ all will come to life again.

PSALM 85 (84)

Lord, you loved your land,
brought Jacob back,
forgot our guilt,
forgave our sins,
swallowed your anger,
your blazing anger.

Bring us back,
saving God.
End your wrath.
Will it stop,
or drag on for ever?

Turn, revive us,
nourish our joy.
Show us mercy.
Save us, Lord!

I listen to God speaking:
"I, the Lord, speak peace,
peace to my faithful people

who turn their hearts to me."
Salvation is coming near,
glory is filling our land.

Love and fidelity embrace;
peace and justice kiss.
Fidelity sprouts from the earth;
justice leans down from heaven.

The Lord pours out riches;
our land springs to life.
Justice clears God's way
justice points the way.

(silent reflection)

PSALM 97 (96)

The Lord rules: the earth is eager,
joy touches distant lands.
God is wrapped in thunder cloud,
throned on justice, throned on right.

Fire marches out in front
and burns up all resistance.
Overhead, God's lightning flares;
the earth shudders to see it.

Mountains melt down like wax
before the Lord, the ruler of all.
Overhead God's justice resounds,
a glory all people can see.

Idolators are the fools,
they brag of empty gods.
You gods, be subject to the Lord!
Zion hears, and is happy.

The cities of Judah are joyful
about your judgments, Lord.

You, Lord, you reach high
in majesty above the earth,
far higher than any god.
Those who love the Lord hate evil;
God shields their faithful lives
and breaks the hold of the wicked.

Light will rain down on the just,
joy on the loyal heart.
Be joyous in the Lord God,
you people of faith,
praise God's holy name!

Glory be . . . .

(Repeat antiphon)

READING   [Isa 53:3-5, 10b, 12]

He was despised and rejected by others;
    a man of suffering and acquainted with infirmity;
and as one from whom others hide their faces
    he was despised, and we held him of no account.
Surely he has borne our infirmities
    and carried our diseases;
yet we accounted him stricken,
    struck down by God, and afflicted.
But he was wounded for our transgressions,
    crushed for our iniquities;
upon him was the punishment that made us whole,
    and by his bruises we are healed.

When you make his life an offering for sin,
    he shall see his offspring, and shall prolong his
        days;
through him the will of the LORD shall prosper.
Therefore I will allot him a portion with the great,
    and he shall divide the spoil with the strong;
because he poured out himself to death,
    and was numbered with the transgressors;
yet he bore the sin of many,
    and made intercession for the transgressors.

(silent reflection)

BENEDICTUS ANTIPHON

Christ must reign until God has put all enemies
under his feet, and the last enemy to be destroyed
is death.

BENEDICTUS

Praise the Lord, the God of Israel,
who shepherds the people and sets them free.

God raises from David's house
a child with power to save.
Through the holy prophets
God promised in ages past
to save us from enemy hands,
from the grip of all who hate us.

The Lord favored our ancestors
recalling the sacred covenant,
the pledge to our ancestor Abraham,
to free us from our enemies,

so we might worship without fear
and be holy and just all our days.

And you, child, will be called
Prophet of the Most High,
for you will come to prepare
a pathway for the Lord
by teaching the people salvation
through forgiveness of their sin.

Out of God's deepest mercy
a dawn will come from on high,
light for those shadowed by death,
a guide for our feet on the way to peace.

Glory be . . . .

(Repeat Benedictus antiphon)

INTERCESSIONS

Our Father . . . .

Gracious and loving God, your Son Jesus has become
your presence among us. Not as a person of power
and strength have you been revealed, but as the
suffering servant, the gentle healer. Give us the
courage to share through patience in his sufferings
so that we might also share in the kingdom where
he lives and reigns with you and the Spirit forever.
Amen.

May God bless us and keep us. May God smile
upon us and be gracious to us. May God look upon
us kindly and give us peace. Amen.

Let us bless God/ and give thanks.

COMMON FOR FEASTS OF CHRIST
EVENING PRAISE

O God, come to my assistance/ make haste to help
me. Glory be . . . .

ANTIPHON

He was known to be of human estate, and it was
thus that he humbled himself, obediently accepting
even death, death on a cross.

PSALM 47 (46)

All peoples, clap your hands,
shout your joy to God.
For God Most High is awesome,
great king of all the earth.

The One who conquers peoples
and sets them at our feet
chooses for beloved Jacob
a land to be our pride.

God ascends the mountain
to cheers and trumpet blasts.
Sing out your praise to God,
to the king, sing out your praise.

For God rules the earth;
sing praise with all your skill.
God rules over nations,
high on the sacred throne.

Foreign rulers join
the people of Abraham's God;
all the powers on earth
belong to God on high.

(silent reflection)

PSALM 93 (92)

Lord, you reign with glory,
draped in splendor, girt with power.
The world stands firm,
not to be shaken,
for your throne, ageless God,
has stood from of old.

Onward roll the waves, O God,
onward like thunder,
onward like fury.
Thundering above the waters,
high above the ocean breakers,
you, God, rise with might.

Your decrees stand unshaken;
the beauty of holiness
fills your house for ever, Lord.

(silent reflection)

PSALM 98

Sing to the Lord a new song,
the Lord of wonderful deeds.
Right hand and holy arm
brought victory to God.

God made that victory known,
revealed justice to nations,
remembered a merciful love
loyal to the house of Israel.
The ends of the earth have seen
the victory of our God.

Shout to the Lord, you earth,
break into song, into praise!
Sing praise to God with a harp,
with a harp and sound of music.
With sound of trumpet and horn,
shout to the Lord, our king.

Let the sea roar with its creatures,
the world and all that live there!
Let rivers clap their hands,
the hills ring out their joy!

The Lord our God comes,
comes to rule the earth,
justly to rule the world,
to govern the peoples aright.

Glory be . . . .

(Repeat antiphon)

READING   [1 Cor 15:20-26]

Christ has been raised from the dead, the first
fruits of those who have died. For since death came
through a human being, the resurrection of the dead
has also come through a human being; for as all die
in Adam, so all will be made alive in Christ. But
each in their own order: Christ the first fruits, then at
his coming those who belong to Christ. Then comes

the end, when he hands over the kingdom to God the Father, after he has destroyed every ruler and every authority and power. For he must reign until he has put all his enemies under his feet. The last enemy to be destroyed is death.

(silent reflection)

MAGNIFICAT ANTIPHON

God highly exalted him, and bestowed on him the name above every other name.

MAGNIFICAT

I acclaim the greatness of the Lord,
I delight in God my Savior,
who regarded my humble state.
Truly from this day on
all ages will call me blest.

For God, wonderful in power,
has used that strength for me.
Holy the name of the Lord!
whose mercy embraces the faithful,
one generation to the next.

The mighty arm of God
scatters the proud in their conceit,
pulls tyrants from their thrones,
and raises up the humble.
The Lord fills the starving
and lets the rich go hungry.

God rescues lowly Israel,
recalling the promise of mercy,

the promise made to our ancestors,
to Abraham's heirs for ever.

Glory be . . . .

(Repeat Magnificat antiphon)

INTERCESSIONS

Our Father . . . .

God who reigns over all, you have brought us all to life in your son Jesus. Keep us in your love, mindful of our death and judgment, sustained by the victory of the risen Christ, that we might labor faithfully and be rewarded with the eternal life you promise, in the name of Jesus our savior. Amen.

May God bless us, deliver us from all evil, and bring us to everlasting life. Amen.

Let us bless God/ and give thanks.

COMMON FOR FEASTS OF MARY
MORNING PRAISE

O God, open my lips,/ and my mouth shall declare
your praise. Glory be . . . .

Hail Mary, full of grace. God is with you.

PSALM 87 (86)

Zion is set on the holy mountain.
The Lord loves her gates
above all the dwellings of Israel.
Great is your renown, city of God.

I register as her citizens
Egypt and Babylon,
Philistia, Ethiopia, and Tyre:
"Each one was born in her."

People will say: "Zion mothered
each and every one."
The Most High protects the city.

God records in the register,
"This one was born here."
Then people will dance and sing,
"My home is here!"

(silent reflection)

PSALM 45

A great song fills my heart,
I will recite it to the king,
my tongue as skilled as the scribal pen.

Unrivaled in beauty,
gracious in speech—
how God has blessed you!

Hero, take up your sword,
majestic in your armor.
Ride on for truth,
show justice to the poor,
wield your power boldly.

Your weapons are ready;
nations fall beneath your might,
your enemies lose heart.

Your throne is as lasting
as the everlasting God.
Integrity is the law of your land.

Because you love justice and hate evil,
God, your God, anoints you
above your peers with festive oil.

Your clothes are fragrant
with myrrh and aloes
and cinnamon flowers.
Music of strings welcomes you
to the ivory palace
and lifts your heart.

Royal women honor you.
On your right hand the queen,
wearing gold of Ophir.

Mark these words, daughter:
leave your family behind,
forget your father's house.

The king desires your beauty.
He is your lord.

Tyre comes with gifts,
the wealthy honor you.

The robes of the queen
are embroidered with gold.
In brilliant attire
she is led to the king;
her attendants follow.
In high spirits
they enter the royal palace.

Your sons will inherit
the throne your fathers held.
They shall reign throughout the land.

Every age will recall your name.
This song will fix it in their memory.

Glory be . . . .

(Repeat antiphon)

READING   [Song 2:1, 3-4, 10-12]

I am a rose of Sharon, a lily of the valleys.
As an apple tree among the trees of the wood,
    so is my beloved among young men.
With great delight I sat in his shadow,
    and his fruit was sweet to my taste.
He brought me to the banqueting house,
    and his intention toward me was love.

My beloved speaks and says to me:
"Arise, my love, my fair one,
    and come away;
for now the winter is past,
    the rain is over and gone.
The flowers appear on the earth;
    the time of singing has come,
and the voice of the turtledove
    is heard in the land."

(silent reflection)

BENEDICTUS ANTIPHON

God who is mighty has done great things for me.

BENEDICTUS

Praise the Lord, the God of Israel,
who shepherds the people and sets them free.

God raises from David's house
a child with power to save.
Through the holy prophets
God promised in ages past
to save us from enemy hands,
from the grip of all who hate us.

The Lord favored our ancestors
recalling the sacred covenant,
the pledge to our ancestor Abraham,
to free us from our enemies,
so we might worship without fear
and be holy and just all our days.

And you, child, will be called
Prophet of the Most High,

for you will come to prepare
a pathway for the Lord
by teaching the people salvation
through forgiveness of their sin.

Out of God's deepest mercy
a dawn will come from on high,
light for those shadowed by death,
a guide for our feet on the way to peace.

Glory be . . . .

(Repeat Benedictus antiphon)

INTERCESSIONS

Our Father . . . .

God our Beloved, you call to each of us with the
ardor of your love, as once you called Mary to give
birth to Jesus, your Son. May her example of trust,
holiness and acceptance of your will inspire us. Fill
us with desire for you through the power of Jesus
and the Holy Spirit. Amen.

May God bless us and keep us. May God smile
upon us and be gracious to us. May God look upon
us kindly and give us peace.

Let us bless God/ and give thanks.

COMMON FOR FEASTS OF MARY
EVENING PRAISE

O God, come to my assistance,/ make haste to help
me. Glory be . . . .

ANTIPHON

Blest is she who trusts that God's words to her will
be fulfilled.

PSALM 48 (47)

Our great Lord
deserves great praise
in the city of God:

Holy mountain, beautiful height,
crown of the earth!

Zion, highest of sacred peaks,
city of the Great King!
God enthroned in its palaces
becomes our sure defense!

Watch the foreign kings
massing to attack;
seeing what they face,
they flee in terror.

Trembling grips them,
anguish like childbirth,
fury like an east wind
shattering a merchant fleet.

What we see
matches what we were told,
"This is the city the Lord protects;
our God strong for ever."
In your temple, Lord,
we recall your constant love.

Your praise, like your name,
fills the whole world.
Your right hand holds the victory.
Mount Zion and the cities of Judah
rejoice at your justice.

March around Zion,
make the circuit,
count each tower.
Ponder these walls,
observe these citadels,

so you may tell your children:
"Here is God!
Our God for ever!
God who leads us
even against death!"

(silent reflection)

PSALM 100 (99)

Shout joy to the Lord, all earth,
serve the Lord with gladness,
enter God's presence with joy!

Know that the Lord is God,
our maker to whom we belong,
our shepherd, and we the flock.

Enter the temple gates,
the courtyard with thanks and praise;
give thanks and bless God's name.

Indeed the Lord is good!
God's love is for ever,
faithful from age to age.

Glory be . . . .

(Repeat antiphon)

READING   [Sir 24:1, 3, 8, 12, 16, 17-22]

Wisdom praises herself, and tells of her glory in the
     midst of her people.
"I came forth from the mouth of the Most High,
     and covered the earth like a mist.
Then the Creator of all things gave me a command,
     and my Creator chose the place for my tent.
God said, 'Make your dwelling in Jacob,
     and in Israel receive your inheritance.'
I took root in an honored people,
     in the portion of the Lord.
Like a terebinth I spread out my branches,
     and my branches are glorious and graceful.
Like the vine I bud forth delights,
     and my blossoms become glorious and abundant
          fruit.
Come to me, you who desire me,
     and eat your fill of my fruits.
Those who eat of me will hunger for more,
     and those who drink of me will thirst for more.
Whoever obeys me will not be put to shame,
     and those who work with me will not sin."

(silent reflection)

MAGNIFICAT ANTIPHON

My being proclaims the greatness of God.

MAGNIFICAT

**I acclaim the greatness of the Lord,
I delight in God my Savior,
who regarded my humble state.
Truly from this day on
all ages will call me blest.**

**For God, wonderful in power,
has used that strength for me.
Holy the name of the Lord!
whose mercy embraces the faithful,
one generation to the next.**

**The mighty arm of God
scatters the proud in their conceit,
pulls tyrants from their thrones,
and raises up the humble.
The Lord fills the starving
and lets the rich go hungry.**

**God rescues lowly Israel,
recalling the promise of mercy,
the promise made to our ancestors,
to Abraham's heirs for ever.**

Glory be . . . .

(Repeat Magnificat antiphon)

INTERCESSIONS

Our Father . . . .

Maker of all, you entered our world to save us and you continue to feed us with the rich fruit of your love. Take root in your people that we may respond wholeheartedly to your will, as Mary did, even when it is difficult to understand. Grant this, Spirit of Wisdom, through Jesus the Christ. Amen.

May God bless us, deliver us from all evil, and bring us to everlasting life. Amen.

Let us bless God/ and give thanks.

COMMON OF APOSTLES
AND MARTYRS
MORNING PRAISE

O God, open my lips,/ and my mouth will declare your praise. Glory be . . . .

ANTIPHON

(Apostles):   **I give you a new commandment: Love one another.**

(Martyrs):   **Live on in me, as I do in you.**

PSALM 116 (114, 115)

I am filled with love,
for the Lord hears me;
the Lord bends to my voice
whenever I call.

Death had me in its grip,
the grave's trap was set,
grief held me fast.
I cried out for God,
"Please, Lord, rescue me!"

Kind and faithful is the Lord,
gentle is our God.
The Lord shelters the poor,
raises me from the dust.
Rest once more, my heart,
for you know the Lord's love.

God rescues me from death,
wiping my tears,
steadying my feet.
I walk with the Lord
in the land of the living.

I believe, even as I say,
"I am afflicted."
I believe, even though I scream,
"Everyone lies!"

What gift can ever repay
God's gift to me?
I raise the cup of freedom
as I call on God's name!
I fulfill my vows to you, Lord,
standing before your assembly.

Lord, you hate to see
your faithful ones die.
I beg you, Lord, hear me:
it is I, the servant you love,
I, the child of your servant.
You freed me from death's grip.

I bring a gift of thanks,
as I call on your name.
I fulfill my vows to you, Lord,
standing before your assembly,
in the courts of your house,
within the heart of Jerusalem.

Hallelujah!

(silent reflection)

PSALM 138 (137)

I thank you with all I am,
I join heaven's chorus.
I bow toward your holy temple,
to praise your name.

By your love and fidelity,
you display to all
the glory of your name and promise.
As soon as I call, you act,
renewing my strength.

Around the world,
rulers praise you
for your commanding word.
They sing of your ways,
"Great is your glory, Lord."

Though high up,
you see the lowly;
though far away,
you keep an eye on the proud.

When I face an opponent,
you keep me alive.
You reach out your hand,
your right hand saves me.

Lord, take up my cause,
your love lasts for ever.
Do not abandon
what your hands have made.

Glory be . . . .

(Repeat antiphon)

READING   [Rom 5:1-8]

Since we are justified by faith, we have peace
with God through our Lord Jesus Christ, through
whom we have obtained access to this grace in which
we stand; and we boast in our hope of sharing the
glory of God. And not only that, but we also boast
in our sufferings, knowing that suffering produces
endurance, and endurance produces character, and
character produces hope, and hope does not disap-
point us, because God's love has been poured into
our hearts through the Holy Spirit that has been given
to us.

For while we were still weak, at the right time
Christ died for the ungodly. Indeed, rarely will anyone die for a righteous person—though perhaps for
a good person someone might actually dare to die.
But God proves his love for us in that while we still
were sinners Christ died for us.

(silent reflection)

BENEDICTUS ANTIPHON

(Apostles):   **As I have done, so you must do.**

(Martyrs):   **If any would serve me, let them follow
me.**

BENEDICTUS

Praise the Lord, the God of Israel,
who shepherds the people and sets them free.

God raises from David's house
a child with power to save.

Through the holy prophets
God promised in ages past
to save us from enemy hands,
from the grip of all who hate us.

The Lord favored our ancestors
recalling the sacred covenant,
the pledge to our ancestor Abraham,
to free us from our enemies,
so we might worship without fear
and be holy and just all our days.

And you, child, will be called
Prophet of the Most High,
for you will come to prepare
a pathway for the Lord
by teaching the people salvation
through forgiveness of their sin.

Out of God's deepest mercy
a dawn will come from on high,
light for those shadowed by death,
a guide for our feet on the way to peace.

Glory be . . . .

(Repeat Benedictus antiphon)

INTERCESSIONS

Our Father . . . .

Source of strength and courage, you gave your
beloved apostle/martyr (name) the conviction of
faith to the very end. Grace us with the ability to
translate your teachings into action, remain patient
amid hardship and live as your true and faithful

servants. We ask this, O God, through Christ our Lord and the Holy Spirit, one God forever and ever. Amen.

May God bless us and keep us. May God smile upon us and be gracious to us. May God look upon us kindly and give us peace. Amen.

Let us bless God/ and give thanks.

COMMON OF APOSTLES
AND MARTYRS
EVENING PRAISE

O God, come to my assistance,/ make haste to help me. Glory be . . . .

ANTIPHON

(Apostles):   **To them I have revealed your name, and I will continue to reveal it.**

(Martyrs):   **If you would be my disciple, take up your cross and follow me.**

PSALM 30 (29)

I give you high praise,
for you, Lord, raised me up
above my gloating enemy.
Lord, how I begged you,
and you, God, healed me.
You pulled me from the pit,
brought me back from Sheol.

Celebrate, all you saints,
praise this awesome God,
whose anger passes quickly,
whose mercy lasts a lifetime—
as laughter fills a day
after one brief night of tears.

When all was going well,
I thought I could never fall;

with God's powerful blessing,
I would stand like a mountain!
Then you hid your face;
I shook with fear!

I cried out, "Lord, Lord!"
I begged, I pleaded:
"What good is my blood to you?
Why push me down the pit?
Can dead bones praise you,
recount your unbroken love?
Listen to me, O God,
turn and help me now."

You changed my anguish
into this joyful dance,
pulled off my sackcloth,
gave me bright new robes,
that my life might sing your glory,
never silent in your praise.
For ever I will thank you,
O Lord, my God.

(silent reflection)

PSALM 144 (143)

Praise God, God my rock
who trains my hands for battle,
my arms for war.

God, my love, my safety,
my stronghold and defender,
God, my shield, my refuge,
you give me victory.

Who are we that you care for us?
Why give a thought to mortals?
We are little more than breath;
our days, fleeting shadows.

Come, Lord, lower the heavens,
touch the mountains,
let them spew out smoke.
Strike lightning,
let your arrows fly,
scatter my enemies in terror.

Reach down from the heavens,
snatch me from crashing waves;
rescue me from strangers
who speak lies
and then swear to them.

I sing you a new song, Lord,
I play my ten-stringed harp,
for you give victory to kings,
you rescue your servant, David.

Save me from the bitter sword,
deliver me from strangers,
who speak lies
and then swear to them.

God, you shape our sons
like tall, sturdy plants;
you sculpt our daughters
like pillars for a palace.

You fill our barns
with all kinds of food,
you bless our fields

with sheep by the thousands
and fatten all our cattle.

There is no breach in the walls,
no outcry in the streets, no exile.
We are a people blest with these gifts,
blest with the Lord as our God!

Glory be . . . .

(Repeat antiphon)

READING   [2 Cor 4:5-11]

We do not proclaim ourselves; we proclaim Jesus
Christ as Lord and ourselves as your slaves for Jesus'
sake. For it is the God who said, "Let light shine out
of darkness," who has shone in our hearts to give the
light of the knowledge of the glory of God in the
face of Jesus Christ.

But we have this treasure in clay jars, so that it
may be made clear that this extraordinary power
belongs to God and does not come from us. We are
afflicted in every way, but not crushed; perplexed,
but not driven to despair; persecuted, but not for-
saken; struck down, but not destroyed; always carrying in the body the death of Jesus, so that the life of
Jesus may also be made visible in our bodies. For
while we live, we are always being given up to death
for Jesus' sake, so that the life of Jesus may be made
visible in our mortal flesh.

(silent reflection)

MAGNIFICAT ANTIPHON

(Apostles):   Whatever you ask God will be given
you in my name.

(Martyrs): **They have washed their robes and made them white in the blood of the Lamb.**

MAGNIFICAT

I acclaim the greatness of the Lord,
I delight in God my Savior,
who regarded my humble state.
Truly from this day on
all ages will call me blest.

For God, wonderful in power,
has used that strength for me.
Holy the name of the Lord!
whose mercy embraces the faithful,
one generation to the next.

The mighty arm of God
scatters the proud in their conceit,
pulls tyrants from their thrones,
and raises up the humble.
The Lord fills the starving
and lets the rich go hungry.

God rescues lowly Israel,
recalling the promise of mercy,
the promise made to our ancestors,
to Abraham's heirs for ever.

Glory be . . . .

(Repeat Magnificat antiphon)

INTERCESSIONS

Our Father . . . .

Light of the world, what we do not possess by nature, you can supply by grace. Inspired by the example of your saints, may we witness courageously to the world the Christ-life that is within us. Hear us, Creator, Redeemer, and Spirit. Amen.

May God bless us, deliver us from all evil, and bring us to everlasting life. Amen.

Let us bless God/ and give thanks.

COMMON OF HOLY MEN
AND WOMEN
MORNING PRAISE

O God, open my lips/ and my mouth shall declare your praise. Glory be . . . .

ANTIPHON

God who has begun the good work in you will carry it through to completion.

(Benedictine saints): **Let us prefer nothing to the love of Christ.**

PSALM 34 (33)

**I will never stop thanking God,
with constant words of praise.
My soul will boast of God;
the poor will hear me and be glad.**

**Join me in praising the Lord;
together tell of God's name.
I asked and the Lord responded,
freed me from all my fears.**

**Turn to God, be bright with joy;
you shall never be let down.
I begged and God heard,
took my burdens from me.**

God's angel defends the faithful,
guards them on every side.
Drink in the richness of God,
enjoy the strength of the Lord.

Live in awe of God, you saints:
you will want for nothing.
Even if lions go hungry,
those seeking God are fed.

Come to me, children, listen:
learn to cherish the Lord.
Do you long for life,
for time to enjoy success?

Keep your tongue from evil,
keep lies far from your lips.
Shun evil, go after good,
press on, seek after peace.

God confronts the wicked
to blot them out for ever,
but turns toward the just
to hear their cry for help.

The troubled call out; God hears,
saves them from all distress.
God stays near broken hearts,
heals the wounded spirit.

The good endure great trials,
but God comes to their rescue
and guards their every bone
so not one is broken.

Evil kills its own kind,
dooms the wicked to death.

**God saves those who keep faith;
no trusting soul is doomed.**

(silent reflection)

PSALM 103 (102)

**My soul, bless the Lord,
Bless God's holy name!
My soul, bless the Lord,
hold dear all God's gifts!**

**Bless God, who forgives your sin
and heals every illness,
who snatches you from death
and enfolds you with tender care,
who fills your life with richness
and gives you an eagle's strength.**

**The Lord, who works justice
and defends the oppressed,
teaches Moses and Israel
divine ways and deeds.**

**The Lord is tender and caring,
slow to anger, rich in love.
God will not accuse us long,
nor bring our sins to trial,
nor exact from us in kind
what our sins deserve.**

**As high as heaven above earth,
so great is God's love for believers.
As far as east from west,
so God removes our sins.**

As tender as father to child,
so gentle is God to believers.
God knows how we are made,
remembers we are dust.

Our days pass by like grass,
our prime like a flower in bloom.
A wind comes, the flower goes,
empty now its place.

God's love is from all ages,
God's justice beyond all time
for believers of each generation:
those who keep the covenant,
who take care to live the law.

The Lord reigns from heaven,
rules over all there is.
Bless the Lord, you angels,
strong and quick to obey,
attending to God's word.

Bless the Lord, you powers,
eager to serve God's will.
Bless the Lord, you creatures,
everywhere under God's rule.
My soul, bless the Lord!

Glory be . . . .

(Repeat antiphon)

READING   [Wis 6:12-19]

Wisdom is radiant and unfading,
and she is easily discerned by those who love her,
and is found by those who seek her.

She hastens to make herself known to those who
    desire her.
One who rises early to seek her will have no difficulty,
for she will be found sitting at the gate.
To fix one's thought on her is perfect understanding,
and one who is vigilant on her account will soon be
    free from care,
because she goes about seeking those worthy of her,
and she graciously appears to them in their paths,
and meets them in every thought.
The beginning of wisdom is the most sincere desire
    for instruction,
and concern for instruction is love of her,
and love of her is the keeping of her laws,
and giving heed to her laws is assurance of immor-
    tality,
and immortality brings one near to God.

(silent reflection)

BENEDICTUS ANTIPHON

The life I live now is not my own; Christ is living
in me.

(Benedictine saints):   We shall run on the path of
God's commandments, our hearts overflowing with
the inexpressible delight of love.

BENEDICTUS

Praise the Lord, the God of Israel,
who shepherds the people and sets them free.

God raises from David's house
a child with power to save.
Through the holy prophets
God promised in ages past
to save us from enemy hands,
from the grip of all who hate us.

The Lord favored our ancestors
recalling the sacred covenant,
the pledge to our ancestor Abraham,
to free us from our enemies,
so we might worship without fear
and be holy and just all our days.

And you, child, will be called
Prophet of the Most High,
for you will come to prepare
a pathway for the Lord
by teaching the people salvation
through forgiveness of their sin.

Out of God's deepest mercy
a dawn will come from on high,
light for those shadowed by death,
a guide for our feet on the way to peace.

Glory be . . . .

(Repeat Benedictus antiphon)

INTERCESSIONS

Our Father . . . .

Holy Wisdom, you seek and meet your beloved
ones. Like your friend *(name)*, may we joyfully run
towards you and do what will profit us so that we,

too, may know your embrace. Grant us this grace,
O Holy Trinity. Amen.

May God bless us and keep us. May God smile
upon us and be gracious to us. May God look upon
us kindly and give us peace. Amen.

Let us bless God/ and give thanks.

COMMON OF HOLY MEN
AND WOMEN
EVENING PRAISE

O God, come to my assistance/ make haste to help me. Glory be . . . .

Be strong. Do everything with love.

(Benedictine saints):   God, in loving kindness, shows us the way of life.

PSALM 115 (113)

Not to us, Lord, not to us,
but to your name give glory,
because of your love,
because of your truth.

Why do the nations say:
"Where is their God?"
Our God is in the heavens
and answers to no one.

Their gods are crafted by hand,
mere silver and gold,
with mouths that are mute,
with ears that are deaf
and noses that cannot smell.

Their hands cannot feel,
their feet cannot walk,

their throats are silent.
Their makers, their worshipers
will be just like them.

Let Israel trust God,
their help and shield.
Let the house of Aaron trust God,
their help and shield.
Let all believers trust God,
their help and shield.

The Lord has remembered us
and will bless us,
will bless the house of Israel,
will bless the house of Aaron.
God will bless all believers,
the small and the great.

May God bless you more and more,
bless all your children.
May you truly be blest
by the maker of heaven and earth.

To the Lord belong the heavens,
to us the earth below!
The dead sing no Hallelujah,
nor do those in the silent ground.
But we will bless you, Lord,
now and for ever.

Hallelujah!

(silent reflection)

PSALM 145 (144)

I will exalt you, God, my king,
for ever bless your name.

I will bless you every day,
for ever praise your name.

Great is the Lord, highly to be praised,
great beyond our reach.

Age to age proclaims your works,
recounts your mighty deeds.
I ponder your splendor and glory
and all your wonderful works.

They reveal your fearful power,
I tell of your great deeds.
They recall your ample goodness,
joyfully sing your justice.

Gracious and merciful is the Lord,
slow to anger, full of love.
The Lord is good in every way,
merciful to every creature.

Let your works praise you, Lord,
your faithful ones bless you.
Let them proclaim your glorious reign,
let them tell of your might.

Let them make known to all
your might and glorious reign.
Your dominion lasts for ever,
your rule for all generations!

The Lord is faithful in every word,
and gracious in every work.
The Lord supports the fallen,
raises those bowed down.

The eyes of all look to you,
you give them food in due time.

You open wide your hand
to feed all living things.

The Lord is just in every way,
loving in every deed.
The Lord is near to those who call,
who cry out from their hearts.

God grants them their desires,
hears their cry and saves them.
Those who love God are kept alive;
the wicked, the Lord destroys.

I will sing the Lord's praise,
all flesh will bless God's Name,
holy, both now and for ever.

Glory be . . . .

(Repeat antiphon)

READING   [1 Cor 13:1-7]

If I speak in the tongues of mortals and of angels,
but do not have love, I am a noisy gong or a clanging
cymbal. And if I have prophetic powers, and understand all mysteries and all knowledge, and if I have
all faith, so as to remove mountains, but do not have
love, I am nothing. If I give away all my possessions,
and if I hand over my body so that I may boast, but
do not have love, I gain nothing.

Love is patient; love is kind; love is not envious
or boastful or arrogant or rude. It does not insist on
its own way; it is not irritable or resentful; it does
not rejoice in wrongdoing, but rejoices in the truth.

It bears all things, believes all things, hopes all things, endures all things.

(silent reflection)

MAGNIFICAT ANTIPHON

Thanks be to God who has given us victory through our Lord, Jesus Christ.

(Benedictine saints):   Let us open our eyes to the light that comes from God.

MAGNIFICAT

I acclaim the greatness of the Lord,
I delight in God my Savior,
who regarded my humble state.
Truly from this day on
all ages will call me blest.

For God, wonderful in power,
has used that strength for me.
Holy the name of the Lord!
whose mercy embraces the faithful,
one generation to the next.

The mighty arm of God
scatters the proud in their conceit,
pulls tyrants from their thrones,
and raises up the humble.
The Lord fills the starving
and lets the rich go hungry.

God rescues lowly Israel,
recalling the promise of mercy,
the promise made to our ancestors,
to Abraham's heirs for ever.

Glory be . . . .

(Repeat Magnificat antiphon)

Intercessions

Our Father . . . .

God, you show us the many faces of love. People our world with lovers, with peacemakers, and fill us with the single-heartedness of your saints. Strengthen us through your Son, Jesus, and the Holy Spirit. Amen.

May God bless us, deliver us from all evil, and bring us to everlasting life. Amen.

Let us bless God/ and give thanks.

COMPLINE
(NIGHT PRAYER)

O God, come to my assistance,/ make haste to help
me. Glory be . . . .

PSALM 4

Answer when I call, faithful God.
You cleared away my trouble;
be good to me, listen to my prayer.

How long, proud fools,
will you insult my honor,
loving lies and chasing shadows?
Look! God astounds believers,
the Lord listens when I call.

Tremble, but do not despair.
Attend to your heart,
be calm through the night,
worship with integrity,
trust in the Lord.

Cynics ask, "Who will bless us?
Even God has turned away."
You give my heart more joy
than all their grain and wine.
I sleep secure at night,
you keep me in your care.

(silent reflection)

PSALM 91 (90)

All you sheltered by the Most High,
who live in Almighty God's shadow,
say to the Lord, "My refuge, my fortress,
my God in whom I trust!"

God will free you from hunters' snares,
will save you from deadly plague,
will cover you like a nesting bird.
God's wings will shelter you.

No nighttime terror shall you fear,
no arrows shot by day,
no plague that prowls the dark,
no wasting scourge at noon.

A thousand may fall at your side,
ten thousand at your right hand.
But you shall live unharmed:
God is sturdy armor.

You have only to open your eyes
to see how the wicked are repaid.
You have the Lord as refuge,
have made the Most High your stronghold.

No evil shall ever touch you,
no harm come near your home.
God instructs angels
to guard you wherever you go.

With your hands they support you
so your foot will not strike a stone.
You will tread on lion and viper,
trample tawny lion and dragon.

"I deliver all who cling to me,
raise the ones who know my name,
answer those who call me,
stand with those in trouble.
These I rescue and honor,
satisfy with long life,
and show my power to save."

(silent reflection)

PSALM 134 (133)

Bless the Lord,
all who serve in God's house,
who stand watch
throughout the night.

Lift up your hands
in the holy place
and bless the Lord.

And may God,
the maker of earth and sky,
bless you from Zion.

Glory be . . . .

(A verse or short reading from Scripture may be inserted here.)

CANTICLE OF SIMEON

Lord, let your servant
now die in peace
for you kept your promise.

With my own eyes
I see the salvation
you prepared for all peoples:
a light of revelation for the Gentiles
and glory to your people Israel.

May the almighty and merciful God, Creator, Redeemer and Spirit, bless and keep us. Amen.

Grant us a restful night/ and a peaceful end.

May the divine assistance be with us always/ and with our loved ones everywhere.